George Cary Eggleston

American War Ballads and Lyrics

A collection of the songs and ballads of the colonial wars, the revolution, the war of

1812-15, the war with Mexico, and the civil war

George Cary Eggleston

American War Ballads and Lyrics
A collection of the songs and ballads of the colonial wars, the revolution, the war of 1812-15, the war with Mexico, and the civil war

ISBN/EAN: 9783744779579

Printed in Europe, USA, Canada, Australia, Japan

Cover: Foto ©Thomas Meinert / pixelio.de

More available books at **www.hansebooks.com**

A COLLECTION OF THE SONGS AND BALLADS OF THE
COLONIAL WARS, THE REVOLUTION, THE WAR
OF 1812-15, THE WAR WITH MEXICO
AND THE CIVIL WAR

EDITED BY

GEORGE CARY EGGLESTON

VOLUME I.

NEW YORK AND LONDON

G. P. PUTNAM'S SONS

The Knickerbocker Press

The Knickerbocker Press, New York
Electrotyped and Printed by
G. P. Putnam's Sons

CONTENTS

	PAGE
ACKNOWLEDGEMENT.	I
PREFACE AND INTRODUCTION	3
THE COLONIAL WARS	11
LOVEWELL'S FIGHT	13
THE SONG OF BRADDOCK'S MEN	19
THE REVOLUTIONARY WAR	21
LIBERTY TREE	23
FREE AMERICA	25
EMANCIPATION FROM BRITISH DEPENDENCE	28
PAUL REVERE'S RIDE	32
WARREN'S ADDRESS	38
NATHAN HALE	40
THE BALLAD OF NATHAN HALE	43
THE BATTLE OF TRENTON	46
THE FATE OF JOHN BURGOYNE	48
THE PROGRESS OF SIR JACK BRAG	51
WAR AND WASHINGTON	53
COLUMBIA	57
TAXATION OF AMERICA	60
THE BATTLE OF THE KEGS	72

	PAGE
CARMEN BELLICOSUM	77
THE YANKEE MAN-OF-WAR	80
PAUL JONES' VICTORY	83
THE ROYAL ADVENTURER	87
EUTAW SPRINGS	90
AN ANCIENT PROPHECY	92
THE DANCE	94
SONG OF MARION'S MEN	97
HAIL COLUMBIA	102
THE WAR OF 1812–15	105
TRUXTON'S VICTORY	107
THE "CONSTELLATION" AND THE "INSURGENTE"	110
THE WASP'S FROLIC	113
"CONSTITUTION" AND "GUERRIÈRE"	115
THE "UNITED STATES" AND "MACEDONIAN"	118
THE "UNITED STATES" AND "MACEDONIAN"	121
PERRY'S VICTORY	126
YANKEE THUNDERS	128
YE PARLIAMENT OF ENGLAND	131
COMRADES ! JOIN THE FLAG OF GLORY	135
OUR NAVY	136
THE STAR-SPANGLED BANNER	138
SEA AND LAND VICTORIES	141
OLD IRONSIDES	144
THE MEXICAN WAR	147
MONTEREY	149
BUENA VISTA	151

Contents

	PAGE
THE BIVOUAC OF THE DEAD	159
THE CIVIL WAR	165
BROTHER JONATHAN'S LAMENT FOR SISTER CAROLINE	167
THE TWELFTH OF APRIL	170
MEN OF THE NORTH AND WEST	174
RHODE ISLAND TO THE SOUTH	176
OUR COUNTRY'S CALL	178
A CRY TO ARMS	181
THE BANNER OF THE STARS	184
THE FLAG OF THE CONSTELLATION	186
THE STARS AND STRIPES	188
THE BONNIE BLUE FLAG	189
THE STRIPES AND THE STARS	191
DIXIE	193
THE OATH OF FREEDOM	197
CIVIL WAR	200
THE MASSACHUSETTS LINE	202
BETHEL	204
THE CHARGE BY THE FORD	209
MANASSAS	212
UPON THE HILL BEFORE CENTREVILLE	214

ILLUSTRATIONS.

	PAGE
THE STAR-SPANGLED BANNER .	*Frontispiece*
THE COLONIAL WARS . .	11
LOVEWELL'S FIGHT .	14
THE SONG OF BRADDOCK'S MEN .	19
THE REVOLUTIONARY WAR .	21
PAUL REVERE'S RIDE . .	33
THE BALLAD OF NATHAN HALE	43
THE BATTLE OF TRENTON	46
THE FATE OF JOHN BURGOYNE	48
CARMEN BELLICOSUM .	79
THE YANKEE MAN-OF-WAR .	80
PAUL JONES' VICTORY . .	83
SONG OF MARION'S MEN . .	97
THE WAR OF 1812–15 . . .	105

	PAGE
TRUXTON'S VICTORY	107
"CONSTITUTION" AND "GUERRIÈRE"	115
THE STAR-SPANGLED BANNER	139
OLD IRONSIDES	145
THE MEXICAN WAR	147
MONTEREY	149
BUENA VISTA	152
THE CIVIL WAR	165
THE TWELFTH OF APRIL	171
THE BANNER OF THE STARS	184
CIVIL WAR	200
THE MASSACHUSETTS LINE	202
BETHEL	204

Typogravures by W. Kurtz.

ACKNOWLEDGMENT.

———

THE editor of these volumes makes grateful acknowl-
edgment of the courtesy of Messrs. Houghton,
Mifflin, & Co., Harper & Brothers, Ticknor & Co., and
D. Lothrop & Co., in freely permitting him to make use
of poems of which they own the copyright, and of their
other good offices. He feels himself indebted also to the
living authors of many poems here presented, for their
readiness in consenting to the use of their writings, and
for the care that many of them have taken to furnish
him with correct versions of poems commonly printed
in inaccurate forms. He is under special obligations in
this regard to General Albert Pike, who has furnished
a transcript, from his own copy of a rare, privately
printed volume, of the stirring ballad "Buena Vista,"
for which a vain search had been made.

PREFACE AND INTRODUCTION.

IN the preparation of these volumes there has been no attempt at completeness. The literature from which the materials are drawn is much too vast to be compressed into two little volumes like these. The aim has been simply to make the collection fairly representative in character, and to include in it those pieces relating to our several wars which best reflect the spirit of the times that produced them.

The work of selection in such a case must always be difficult and the result more or less unsatisfactory. There are many reasons for this, some of which no one who has not undertaken a task of this kind can fully appreciate. There is no fixed standard of judgment by which to make a certainly just comparative estimate of the quality of several poems, some of which must be taken and the others left. Merit, in the case of war poems, is the composite result of so many different things that no criticism can hope to make an entirely satisfactory qualitative analysis of such literature. The poetic quality of some pieces entitles them to editorial acceptance, quite irrespective of other considerations, while there are other pieces having very little poetic quality, or none at all, whose claim to consideration on other grounds is incontestible. Mr. Stedman's "Wanted—A Man," Mr. William Winter's exquisitely tender poem "After All," Miss Osgood's "Driving Home the Cows," and Mr. George Parsons Lathrop's "Keenan's Charge," may serve as examples of pieces which no editor with the least capacity of poetic appreciation would hesitate to include in such a collection on the ground of merit even if their character were somewhat at variance, as in this case it is not, with the scheme of the collection. On the other hand there are such things as "Three Hundred Thousand More," several of the rude songs of the war of 1812, and many other pieces, which make equally imperative claims to favor on grounds that have no relation to the question of poetic merit.

The song concerning the "Constitution and Guerrière," for example, is very nearly as destitute of poetic quality as metrical writing can be, and yet no editor of a collection like this would think of omitting a piece that had for so many years stirred the hearts of patriots and moved them to rejoice in the achievements of their country's heroes.

The complex nature of the considerations that must determine the choice of poems for inclusion is but one of several difficulties encountered in the execution of such a task as this. In any event, many things must be omitted which merit insertion, and the reader who misses a favorite piece is prompt to point to others which seem to him less worthy, and to ask why these were not made to give place to the one omitted. There are three answers to be made to the challenge of such a reader : first, that his judgment in the matter may be wrong ; second, that the editor, being human, may have erred in his choice ; and third, that in a collection intended to be broadly representative rather than complete, preference must sometimes be given to the less worthy piece which happens to reflect some phase of sentiment not otherwise presented, even at the cost of sacrificing the worthier one which illustrates aspects otherwise sufficiently shown.

So much by way of explanation, not of apology ; for if a book be in need of apology, no apology can be sufficient for it.

In the matter of arrangement the poems naturally fall

into five principal groups. Within the groups the chronology of the events referred to has been adopted as a general rule of arrangement, while for the most part poems that have no reference to particular events or epochs have been placed at the end of the groups to which they belong. No rule of arrangement, however, has been permitted to dominate other considerations where other considerations have seemed the more important.

In presenting the ballads and lyrics of the civil war, it has been thought best not to give those from the North and those from the South in separate groups. There are several objections to such an arrangement, of which it is perhaps sufficient to mention a single one, namely, that by the separation of poems relating to the same events or the same aspects of the struggle, much of their historical significance is lost, and the comparison which the reflective reader naturally wishes to make between the moods, impulses, aspirations, and points of view of the poets on opposite sides is rendered much more difficult and less satisfactory.

It would be a special pity, for example, not to place in juxtaposition Bryant's "Our Country's Call" and Timrod's "A Cry to Arms." An essay of no little value to

the student of the inner springs of history might be
written upon these two poems with their strange simi-
larities and their still stranger contrasts.   Indeed a critic
of creative ability might almost reconstruct the history
of the events which produced the war, and discover the
characters and circumstances and, above all, the points
of view of the people on either side of the contest, by
a study of these two appeals, even if all other sources of
information were lost.   For this and other reasons it has
been thought best to make but a single group of the
poems of the civil war, bringing together all those that
relate to the same or to like subjects, and indicating
the origin of the southern pieces by printing the word
"Southern " at the end of each.

In the South during the civil war, almost all the adult
males, with some who were rather adolescent than adult,
were under arms.   As a consequence, the men who wrote
the poetry of the Southern side were necessarily soldiers.
But in less peculiar circumstances the men who write
the poetry of war, the men who make the songs that
soldiers love to sing, the men who irresistibly stir
patriotism in the blood of youth, the men who embalm
heroic deeds in thrilling verse, and touch all hearts to
pity and all eyes to tears by the tender pathos of their

chronicles of suffering, are not the men who do the fight-
ing.   It was not a soldier who wrote "The Charge of the
Light Brigade," and it was the gentle master of Abbots-
ford that interpreted the daring deeds of knightly times
in song and story.   So in our civil war the most and the
best of the poems, except as the matter was determined
at the South by peculiar circumstances, were the work
of men who were not themselves combatants.   Cynical
reflections have sometimes been indulged in on this
score, but they are unjust and shallow, as cynical re-
flections are apt to be.   The qualities that make one a
poet are not those that make one a soldier.   Sometimes
the two characters are united in one person, but that is
rare ; and the man who has the gift to write the poetry
of a war which involves human liberty as its issue, best
serves the cause by writing it.   His part is as important
as that of the soldier who bears arms, and his influence
upon the result is quite as great.   The patriotism and the
courage of the Greeks owed more to Homer than to the
warriors whose deeds he chronicled, and Paul Revere did
far less for his country by what was after all a common-
place horseback journey, than Longfellow long afterward
did by telling the story of that ride in quite other than
commonplace poetry.

Of the extent to which the war songs and ballads of a people influence the character and destiny of that people, much has been written, and the truth is not yet half told. Our present concern with this literature, however, has less regard to its influence than to its value as historical material. History records the events in a nation's life; poetry, and especially ballad poetry, reflects the character, the aspirations, the passions, and the purposes of a people; and viewed in this light a study of the war ballads and lyrics of our country must fill every reader's mind with hope and courage. Many of the poems presented in these little volumes are rude, some of them being scarcely better than doggerel, while much of the material is poetry of a very high order; but there are certain characteristics common to all the poems, and these are the characteristics that distinguish a virile race which encounters difficulty with stalwart courage and confronts danger with an unruffled mind. It is the poetry of strength and manly self-reliance. There is not a plaint of weakness anywhere in it. It is inspired from beginning to end by a high and unfaltering faith in the truth of the doctrines of human liberty that underlie our entire history and constitute the vital principle of our institutions.

The ruder poems are a trifle truculent now and then perhaps, but some little truculence may be allowed as a poetic license to the poet who sings of his countrymen's prowess in just wars. In preparing this little collection the editor has had occasion to read anew the entire body of American war poetry of the ballad and lyric class, and he ends the examination with a feeling of intense satisfaction in the knowledge that there is not an unmanly or a cowardly line in it and scarcely an ungenerous one.

THE COLONIAL WARS

LOVEWELL'S FIGHT.

[THIS ballad, written in 1725, soon after the battle of May 8th, in that year, was said by a contemporary writer to be "the most beloved song in all New England," though "Chevy Chace" had been known there almost as well as in old England. The name of the author is lost to us, but his work has been preserved in Penhallow's "History of the Wars of New England with the Eastern Indians," 1726. The ballad is rude and destitute of poetic quality; but it has extraordinary interest as the earliest American war ballad known to us as having been dear to the hearts of the people who sang or recited it. It has interest, also, as a reflection of manners. The commendation bestowed upon the chaplain for *scalping* Indians as well as killing them is suggestive.—EDITOR.]

LOVEWELL'S FIGHT.

OF worthy Captain Lovewell, I purpose now to sing,
　　How valiantly he served his country and his king;
He and his valiant soldiers did range the woods full wide,
And hardships they endured to quell the Indian's pride.

'T was nigh unto Pigwacket, on the eighth day of May,
They spied a rebel Indian soon after break of day;
He on a bank was walking, upon a neck of land,
Which leads into a pond as we're made to understand.

14

Our men resolved to have him, and travelled two miles
    round,
Until they met the Indian, who boldly stood his ground;
Then up speaks Captain Lovewell: "Take you good
    heed," says he,
"This rogue is to decoy us, I very plainly see.

"The Indians lie in ambush, in some place nigh at hand,
In order to surround us upon this neck of land;
Therefore we 'll march in order, and each man leave his
    pack;
That we may briskly fight them, when they make their
    attack."

They came unto this Indian, who did them thus defy,
As soon as they came nigh him, two guns he did let fly,
Which wounded Captain Lovewell, and likewise one man
    more,
But when this rogue was running, they laid him in his
    gore.

Then having scalped the Indian, they went back to the
    spot
Where they had laid their packs down, but there they
    found them not.
For the Indians having spied them, when they them
    down did lay,
Did seize them for their plunder, and carry them away.

These rebels lay in ambush, this very place hard by,
So that an English soldier did one of them espy,
And cried out, "Here's an Indian"! with that they
    started out,
As fiercely as old lions, and hideously did shout.

With that our valiant English all gave a loud huzza,
To show the rebel Indians they feared them not a straw :
So now the fight began, and as fiercely as could be,
The Indians ran up to them, but soon were forced to flee.

Then spake up Captain Lovewell, when first the fight
    began :
"Fight on, my valiant heroes ! You see they fall like
    rain."
For as we are informed, the Indians were so thick
A man could scarcely fire a gun and not some of them hit.

Then did the rebels try their best our soldiers to sur-
    round,
But they could not accomplish it, because there was a
    pond,
To which our men retreated, and covered all the rear,
The rogues were forced to face them, although they
    skulked for fear.

Two logs there were behind them that close together lay,
Without being discovered, they could not get away ;

Therefore our valiant English they travelled in a row,
And at a handsome distance, as they were wont to go.

'T was ten o'clock in the morning when first the fight
    begun,
And fiercely did continue until the setting sun ;
Excepting that the Indians some hours before 't was
    night
Drew off into the bushes and ceased awhile to fight.

But soon again returned, in fierce and furious mood.
Shouting as in the morning, but yet not half so loud ;
For as we are informed, so thick and fast they fell,
Scarce twenty of their number at night did get home
    well.

And that our valiant English till midnight there did stay,
To see whether the rebels would have another fray ;
But they no more returning, they made off towards their
    home,
And brought away their wounded as far as they could
    come.

Of all our valiant English there were but thirty-four,
And of the rebel Indians there were about fourscore,
And sixteen of our English did safely home return,
The rest were killed and wounded, for which we all must
    mourn.

Our worthy Captain Lovewell among them there did die,
They killed Lieutenant Robbins, and wounded good
  young Frye,
Who was our English chaplain ; he many Indians slew,
And some of them he scalped when bullets round him
  flew.

Young Fullam, too, I 'll mention, because he fought so
  well,
Endeavoring to save a man, a sacrifice he fell :
But yet our valiant Englishmen in fight were ne'er dis-
  mayed,
But still they kept their motion, and Wymans captain
  made,

Who shot the old chief Pagus, which did the foe defeat,
Then set his men in order, and brought off the retreat ;
And braving many dangers and hardships in the way,
They safe arrived at Dunstable, the thirteenth day of
  May.

THE SONG OF BRADDOCK'S MEN.

Fort DuQuesne Expedition, 1755.

TO arms, to arms! my jolly grena-
    diers!
  Hark how the drums do roll it along!
To horse, to horse, with valiant good
    cheer;
We'll meet our proud foe before it is long.
    Let not your courage fail you;
    Be valiant, stout, and bold;
    And it will soon avail you,
    My loyal hearts of gold.
Huzzah, my valiant countrymen!—again I say huzzah!
'T is nobly done,—the day 's our own—huzzah, huzzah!

March on, march on, brave Braddock leads the foremost;
　　The battle is begun as you may fairly see.
Stand firm, be bold, and it will soon be over;
　　We'll soon gain the field from our proud enemy.
　　　　A squadron now appears, my boys;
　　　　If that they do but stand!
　　　　Boys, never fear, be sure you mind
　　　　The word of command!
Huzzah, my valiant countrymen!—again I say huzzah!
'T is nobly done,—the day's our own—huzzah, huzzah!

See how, see how, they break and fly before us!
　　See how they are scattered all over the plain!
Now, now—now, now, our country will adore us!
　　In peace and in triumph, boys, when we return again!
　　　　Then laurels shall our glory crown
　　　　For all our actions told:
　　　　The hills shall echo all around,
　　　　My loyal hearts of gold.
Huzzah, my valiant countrymen!—again I say huzzah!
'T is nobly done,—the day's our own—huzzah, huzzah!

THE REVOLUTIONARY WAR

LIBERTY TREE.

By THOMAS PAINE.

(Published in the *Pennsylvania Magazine*, 1775.)

IN a chariot of light from the regions of day,
    The Goddess of Liberty came ;
Ten thousand celestials directed the way,
    And hither conducted the dame.
A fair budding branch from the gardens above,
    Where millions with millions agree,
She brought in her hand as a pledge of her love,
    And the plant she named *Liberty Tree*.

The celestial exotic struck deep in the ground,
    Like a native it flourished and bore ;
The fame of its fruit drew the nations around,
    To seek out this peaceable shore.
Unmindful of names or distinction they came,
    For freemen like brothers agree ;
With one spirit endued, they one friendship pursued,
    And their temple was *Liberty Tree*.

Beneath this fair tree, like the patriarchs of old,
    Their bread in contentment they ate,
Unvexed with the troubles of silver and gold,
    The cares of the grand and the great.
With timber and tar they Old England supplied,
    And supported her power on the sea ;
Her battles they fought, without getting a groat,
    For the honor of *Liberty Tree*.

But hear, O ye swains, 't is a tale most profane,
    How all the tyrannical powers,
Kings, Commons, and Lords, are uniting amain,
    To cut down this guardian of ours ;
From the east to the west blow the trumpet to arms,
    Through the land let the sound of it flee,
Let the far and the near, all unite with a cheer,
    In defence of our *Liberty Tree*.

FREE AMERICA.

[This poem first appeared in the newspapers in 1774, and was ascribed to Joseph Warren.—EDITOR.]

THAT seat of Science, Athens,
    And earth's proud mistress, Rome ;
Where now are all their glories ?
We scarce can find a tomb.
Then guard your rights, Americans,
Nor stoop to lawless sway ;
Oppose, oppose, oppose, oppose,
    For North America.

We led fair Freedom hither,
And lo, the desert smiled !
A paradise of pleasure
Was opened in the wild !
Your harvest, bold Americans,
No power shall snatch away !
Huzza, huzza, huzza, huzza,
    For free America.

Torn from a world of tyrants,
Beneath this western sky,
We formed a new dominion,
A land of liberty :
The world shall own we 're masters here ;
Then hasten on the day :
Huzza, huzza, huzza, huzza,
    For free America.

Proud Albion bowed to Cæsar,
And numerous lords before ;
To Picts, to Danes, to Normans,
And many masters more :
But we can boast, Americans,
We 've never fallen a prey ;
Huzza, huzza, huzza, huzza,
    For free America.

God bless this maiden climate,
And through its vast domain
May hosts of heroes cluster,
Who scorn to wear a chain :
And blast the venal sycophant
That dares our rights betray ;
Huzza, huzza, huzza, huzza,
    For free America.

Lift up your hands, ye heroes,
And swear with proud disdain,

The wretch that would ensnare you,
Shall lay his snares in vain :
Should Europe empty all her force,
We 'll meet her in array,
And fight and shout, and shout and fight
    For North America.

Some future day shall crown us,
The masters of the main,
Our fleets shall speak in thunder
To England, France, and Spain ;
And the nations over the ocean spread
Shall tremble and obey
The sons, the sons, the sons, the sons,
    Of brave America.

EMANCIPATION FROM BRITISH DEPENDENCE.

By PHILIP FRENEAU.

[The following note explanatory of references to
proper names, etc., in this poem is copied from Duyc-
kinck's edition of Freneau.—EDITOR.]

NOTE.—Sir James Wallace, Admiral Graves, and Cap-
tain Montague, were British naval officers, employed
on our coast. The *Viper* and *Rose* were vessels in the
service. Lord Dunmore, the last royal governor of Vir-
ginia, had recently, in April, 1775, removed the public
stores from Williamsburg, and, in conjunction with a
party of adherents, supported by the naval force on
the station, was making war on the province. William
Tryon, the last Royal governor of New York, informed
of a resolution of the Continental Congress: "That it
be recommended to the several provincial assemblies
in conventions and councils, or committees of safety,
to arrest and secure every person in their respective

colonies whose going at large may, in their opinion, endanger the safety of the colony or the liberties of America," discerning the signs of the times, took refuge on board the Halifax packet in the harbor, and left the city in the middle of October, 1775.

EMANCIPATION FROM BRITISH DEPENDENCE.

By PHILIP FRENEAU.

Libera nos, Domine—Deliver us, O Lord,
Not only from British dependence, but also,

FROM a junto that labor for absolute power,
    Whose schemes disappointed have made them look
      sour ;
From the lords of the council, who fight against freedom
Who still follow on where delusion shall lead 'em.

From groups at St. James's who slight our Petitions,
And fools that are waiting for further submissions ;
From a nation whose manners are rough and abrupt,
From scoundrels and rascals whom gold can corrupt.

From pirates sent out by command of the king
To murder and plunder, but never to swing ;
From Wallace, and Graves, and *Vipers*, and *Roses*,
Whom, if Heaven pleases, we 'll give bloody noses.

From the valiant Dunmore, with his crew of banditti
Who plunder Virginians at Williamsburg city,
From hot-headed Montague, mighty to swear,
The little fat man with his pretty white hair.

From bishops in Britain, who butchers are grown,
From slaves that would die for a smile from the throne,
From assemblies that vote against Congress' proceedings,
(Who now see the fruit of their stupid misleadings).

From Tryon, the mighty, who flies from our city,
And swelled with importance, disdains the committee;
(But since he is pleased to proclaim us his foes,
What the devil care we where the devil he goes.)

From the caitiff, Lord North, who would bind us in
    chains,
From our noble King Log, with his toothful of brains,
Who dreams, and is certain (when taking a nap)
He has conquered our lands as they lay on his map.

From a kingdom that bullies, and hectors, and swears,
I send up to Heaven my wishes and prayers
That we, disunited, may freemen be still,
And Britain go on—to be damn'd if she will.

1775

PAUL REVERE'S RIDE.

BY HENRY WADSWORTH LONGFELLOW.

LISTEN, my children, and you shall hear
  Of the midnight ride of Paul Revere,
On the eighteenth of April, in Seventy-five;
Hardly a man is now alive
Who remembers that famous day and year.

He said to his friend : " If the British march
By land or sea from the town to-night,
Hang a lantern aloft in the belfry arch
Of the North Church tower as a signal light,—
One, if by land, and two, if by sea ;
And I on the opposite shore will be,
Ready to ride and spread the alarm
Through every Middlesex village and farm,
For the country folk to be up and to arm."

Then he said " Good-night," and with muffled oar
Silently row'd to the Charlestown shore,
Just as the moon rose over the bay,
Where swinging wide at her moorings lay

The *Somerset*, British man-of-war ;
A phantom ship, with each mast and spar
Across the moon like a prison bar,
And a huge black hulk, that was magnified
By its own reflection in the tide.

Meanwhile his friend, through alley and street,
Wanders and watches with eager ears,
Till in the silence around him he hears
The muster of men at the barrack-door,
The sound of arms, and the tramp of feet,
And the measured tread of the grenadiers
Marching down to their boats on the shore.

Then he clim'd the tower of the Old North Church,
By the wooden stairs, with stealthy tread,
To the belfry-chamber overhead,
And startled the pigeons from their perch
On the sombre rafters, that round him made
Masses and moving shapes of shade,—
By the trembling ladder, steep and tall,
To the highest window in the wall,
Where he paused to listen and look down
A moment on the roofs of the town,
And the moonlight flowing over all.

Beneath, in the churchyard lay the dead,
In their night-encampment on the hill,
Wrapp'd in silence so deep and still
That he could hear, like a sentinel's tread,
The watchful night-wind, as it went
Creeping along from tent to tent,
And seeming to whisper, "All is well!"
A moment only he feels the spell

Of the place and the hour, and the secret dread
Of the lonely belfry and the dead ;
For suddenly all his thoughts are bent
On a shadowy something far away,
Where the river widens to meet the bay,—
A line of black that bends and floats
On the rising tide like a bridge of boats.

Meanwhile, impatient to mount and ride,
Booted and spurr'd, with a heavy stride
On the opposite shore walk'd Paul Revere.
Now he patted his horse's side,
Now gazed at the landscape far and near,
Then, impetuous, stamp'd the earth,
And turn'd and tighten'd his saddle-girth ;
But mostly he watch'd with eager search
The belfry-tower of the Old North Church,
As it rose above the graves on the hill,
Lonely and spectral and sombre and still.
And lo ! as he looks, on the belfry's height
A glimmer, and then a gleam of light !
He springs to the saddle, the bridle he turns,
But lingers and gazes, till full on his sight
A second lamp in the belfry burns.

A hurry of hoofs in a village street,
A shape in the moonlight, a bulk in the dark,
And beneath, from the pebbles, in passing a spark
Struck out by a steed flying fearless and fleet ;

That was all; and yet, through the gloom and the light
The fate of a nation was riding that night;
And the spark struck out by that steed in his flight
Kindled the land into flame with its heat.

He has left the village and mounted the steep,
And beneath him, tranquil and broad and deep,
Is the Mystic, meeting the ocean tides,
And under the alders that skirt its edge,
Now soft on the sand, now loud on the ledge,
Is heard the tramp of his steed as he rides.
It was twelve by the village clock
When he cross'd the bridge into Medford town.
He heard the crowing of the cock,
And the barking of the farmer's dog,
And felt the damp of the river's fog,
That rises after the sun goes down.

It was one by the village clock
When he galloped into Lexington.
He saw the gilded weathercock
Swim in the moonlight as he pass'd,
And the meeting-house windows, blank and bare,
Gaze at him with spectral glare,
As if they already stood aghast
At the bloody work they would look upon.

It was two by the village clock
When he came to the bridge in Concord town,

He heard the bleating of the flock,
And the twitter of birds among the trees,
And felt the breath of the morning breeze
Blowing over the meadows brown.
And one was safe and asleep in his bed
Who at the bridge would be first to fall,
Who that day would be lying dead,
Pierced by a British musket-ball.

You know the rest : in the books you have read,
How the British regulars fired and fled,—
How the farmers gave them ball for ball,
From behind each fence and farmyard wall,
Chasing the red-coats down the lane,
Then crossing the fields to emerge again
Under the trees at the turn of the road,
And only pausing to fire and load.

So through the night rode Paul Revere,
And so through the night went his cry of alarm
To every Middlesex village and farm,—
A cry of defiance, and not of fear,
A voice in the darkness, a knock at the door,
And a word that shall echo for evermore !
For, borne on the night-wind of the past,
Through all our history to the last,
In the hour of darkness, and peril, and need,
The people will waken and listen to hear
The hurrying hoof-beats of that steed,
And the midnight message of Paul Revere.

WARREN'S ADDRESS.

BY JOHN PIERPONT.

STAND! the ground's your own, my braves!
    Will ye give it up to slaves?
Will ye look for greener graves?
    Hope ye mercy still?
What's the mercy despots feel?
Hear it in that battle peal!
Read it on yon bristling steel!
    Ask it,—ye who will.

Fear ye foes who kill for hire?
Will ye to your homes retire?
Look behind you!—they 're afire!
    And, before you, see
Who have done it! From the vale
On they come!—and will ye quail?
Leaden rain and iron hail
    Let their welcome be!

In the God of battles trust!
Die we may,—and die we must:

But, oh where can dust to dust
    Be consign'd so well,
As where Heaven its dews shall shed
On the martyr'd patriot's bed,
And the rocks shall raise their head
    Of his deeds to tell?

NATHAN HALE.

By FRANCIS M. FINCH.

TO drum-beat and heart-beat,
    A soldier marches by;
There is color in his cheek,
    There is courage in his eye,
Yet to drum-beat and heart-beat
    In a moment he must die.

By starlight and moonlight,
    He seeks the Briton's camp;
He hears the rustling flag,
    And the armèd sentry's tramp;
And the starlight and moonlight
    His silent wanderings lamp.

With slow tread and still tread,
    He scans the tented line;
And he counts the battery guns,
    By the gaunt and shadowy pine;
And his slow tread and still tread
    Gives no warning sign.

The dark wave, the plumed wave,
   It meets his eager glance;
And it sparkles 'neath the stars,
   Like the glimmer of a lance—
A dark wave, a plumed wave,
   On an emerald expanse.

A sharp clang, a still clang,
   And terror in the sound!
For the sentry, falcon-eyed,
   In the camp a spy hath found;
With a sharp clang, a steel clang,
   The patriot is bound.

With calm brow, steady brow,
   He listens to his doom;
In his look there is no fear,
   Nor a shadow-trace of gloom;
But with calm brow and steady brow
   He robes him for the tomb.

In the long night, the still night,
   He kneels upon the sod;
And the brutal guards withhold
   E'en the solemn word of God!
In the long night, the still night,
   He walks where Christ hath trod.

'Neath the blue morn, the sunny morn,
  He dies upon the tree ;
And he mourns that he can lose
  But one life for Liberty ;
And in the blue morn, the sunny morn,
  His spent wings are free.

But his last words, his message-words,
  They burn, lest friendly eye
Should read how proud and calm
  A patriot could die,
With his last words, his dying words,
  A soldier's battle-cry.

From Fame-leaf and Angel-leaf,
  From monument and urn,
The sad of earth, the glad of heaven,
  His tragic fate shall learn ;
And on Fame-leaf and Angel-leaf
  The name of HALE shall burn !

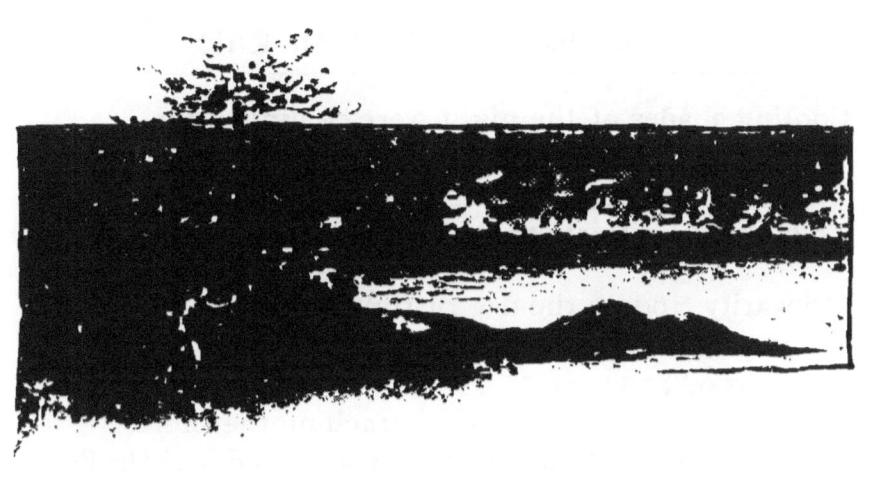

THE BALLAD OF NATHAN HALE.

(Moore's "Songs and Ballads of the American Revolution." 1856.)

THE breezes went steadily through the tall pines,
   A-saying "oh! hu-ush !" a-saying " oh ! hu-ush !"
As stilly stole by a bold legion of horse,
For Hale in the bush, for Hale in the bush.

" Keep still !" said the thrush as she nestled her young
In a nest by the road ; in a nest by the road.
" For the tyrants are near, and with them appear
What bodes us no good, what bodes us no good."

The brave captain heard it, and thought of his home
In a cot by the brook ; in a cot by the brook.
With mother and sister and memories dear,
He so gayly forsook ; he so gayly forsook.

Cooling shades of the night were coming apace,
The tattoo had beat ; the tattoo had beat.
The noble one sprang from his dark lurking-place,
To make his retreat ; to make his retreat.

He warily trod on the dry rustling leaves,
As he passed through the wood, as he passed through the
        wood ;
And silently gained his rude launch on the shore,
As she played with the flood ; as she played with the flood

The guards of the camp, on that dark, dreary night,
Had a murderous will ; had a murderous will.
They took him and bore him afar from the shore,
To a hut on the hill ; to a hut on the hill.

No mother was there, nor a friend who could cheer,
In that little stone cell ; in that little stone cell.
But he trusted in love, from his Father above,
In his heart, all was well ; in his heart, all was well.

An ominous owl, with his solemn bass voice,
Sat moaning hard by ; sat moaning hard by :
" The tyrant's proud minions most gladly rejoice,
For he soon must die; for he soon must die."

The brave fellow told them, no thing he restrained,—
The cruel general ! the cruel general !—
His errand from camp, of the ends to be gained,
And said that was all ; and said that was all.

They took him and bound him and bore him away,
Down the hill's grassy side ; down the hill's grassy side.
'T was there the base hirelings, in royal array,
His cause did deride ; his cause did deride.

Five minutes were given, short moments, no more,
For him to repent ; for him to repent.
He prayed for his mother, he asked not another,
To Heaven he went ; to Heaven he went.

The faith of a martyr the tragedy showed,
As he trod the last stage ; as he trod the last stage.
And Britons will shudder at gallant Hale's blood
As his words do presage, as his words do presage.

" Thou pale king of terrors, thou life's gloomy foe,
Go frighten the slave ; go frighten the slave ;
Tell tyrants, to you their allegiance they owe.
No fears for the brave ; no fears for the brave."

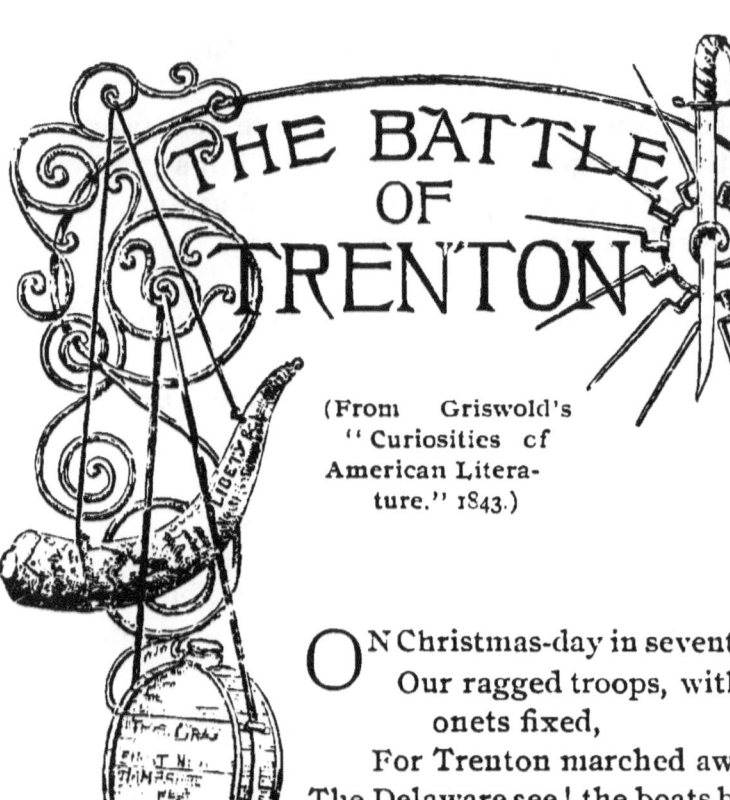

THE BATTLE OF TRENTON

(From Griswold's "Curiosities of American Literature." 1843.)

ON Christmas-day in seventy-six,
  Our ragged troops, with bay-
    onets fixed,
  For Trenton marched away.
The Delaware see! the boats below!
The light obscured by hail and
    snow!
  But no signs of dismay.

Our object was the Hessian band,
That dared invade fair freedom's land,
  And quarter in that place.
Great Washington he led us on,
Whose streaming flag, in storm or sun,
  Had never known disgrace.

46

In silent march we passed the night,
Each soldier panting for the fight,
    Though quite benumbed with frost.
Greene on the left at six began,
The right was led by Sullivan
    Who ne'er a moment lost.

Their pickets stormed, the alarm was spread,
That rebels risen from the dead
    Were marching into town.
Some scampered here, some scampered there,
And some for action did prepare ;
    But soon their arms laid down.

Twelve hundred servile miscreants,
With all their colors, guns, and tents,
    Were trophies of the day.
The frolic o'er, the bright canteen,
In centre, front, and rear was seen
    Driving fatigue away.

Now, brothers of the patriot bands,
Let 's sing deliverance from the hands
    Of arbitrary sway.
And as our life is but a span,
Let 's touch the tankard while we can.
    In memory of that day.

(From Griswold's "Curiosities of American Literature.")

WHEN Jack the king's commander
　　Was going to his duty,
Through all the crowd he smiled and bowed
To every blooming beauty.

The city rung with feats he 'd done
In Portugal and Flanders,
And all the town thought he'd be crowned
The first of Alexanders.

To Hampton Court he first repairs
To kiss great George's hand, sirs ;
Then to harangue on state affairs
Before he left the land, sirs.

The " Lower House " sat mute as mouse
To hear his grand oration ;
And "all the peers," with loudest cheers,
Proclaimed him to the nation.

Then off he went to Canada,
Next to Ticonderoga,
And quitting those away he goes
Straightway to Saratoga.

With great parade his march he made
To gain his wished-for station,
While far and wide his minions hied
To spread his " Proclamation."

To such as stayed he offers made
Of "pardon on submission ;
But savage bands should waste the lands
Of all in opposition."

But ah, the cruel fates of war !
This boasted son of Britain,
When mounting his triumphal car,
With sudden fear was smitten.

The sons of Freedom gathered round,
His hostile bands confounded,
And when they 'd fain have turned their back
They found themselves surrounded!

In vain they fought, in vain they fled ;
Their chief, humane and tender,
To save the rest soon thought it best
His forces to surrender.

Brave St. Clair, when he first retired,
Knew what the fates portended ;
And Arnold and heroic Gates
His conduct have defended.

Thus may America's brave sons
With honor be rewarded,
And be the fate of all her foes
The same as here recorded.

THE PROGRESS OF SIR JACK BRAG.

(McCarty's National Song-Book.)

SAID Burgoyne to his men, as they passed in review,
  Tullalo, tullalo, tullalo, boys!
These rebels their course very quickly will rue,
And fly as the leaves 'fore the autumn tempest flew,
When him who is your leader they know, boys!
    They with men have now to deal,
    And we soon will make them feel—
    Tullalo, tullalo, tullalo, boys!
That a loyal Briton's arm, and a loyal Briton's steel,
Can put to flight a rebel, as quick as other foe, boys!
    Tullalo, tullalo, tullalo,
    Tullalo, tullalo, tullalo-o-o-o, boys!

As to Sa-ra-tog' he came, thinking how to jo the game,
    Tullalo, tullalo, tullalo, boys!
He began to see the grubs, in the branches of his fame,
He began to have the trembles, lest a flash should be the
    flame

For which he had agreed his perfume to forego, boys!
    No lack of skill, but fates,
    Shall make us yield to Gates,
    Tullalo, tullalo, tullalo, boys!
The devils may have leagued, as you know, with the
        States,
But we never will be beat by any mortal foe, boys!
    Tullalo, tullalo, tullalo,
    Tullalo, tullalo, tullalo-o-o-o, boys!

WAR AND WASHINGTON.

(As sung during the Revolution.)

BY JONATHAN MITCHELL SEWARD.

VAIN Britons, boast no longer with proud indignity,
  By land your conquering legions, your matchless
    strength at sea,
Since we, your braver sons incensed, our swords have
  girded on,
Huzza, huzza, huzza, huzza, for war and Washington.

Urged on by North and vengeance those valiant cham-
  pions came,
Loud bellowing Tea and Treason, and George was all on
  flame,
Yet sacrilegious as it seems, we rebels still live on,
And laugh at all their empty puffs, huzza for Washington!

Still deaf to mild entreaties, still blind to England's good,
You have for thirty pieces betrayed your country's blood.
Like Esop's greedy cur you'll gain a shadow for your
  bone,
Yet find us fearful shades indeed inspired by Washington.

53

Mysterious ! unexampled ! incomprehensible!
The blundering schemes of Britain their folly, pride, and
    zeal,
Like lions how ye growl and threat ! mere asses have
    you shown,
And ye shall share an ass's fate, and drudge for Wash-
    ington !

Your dark unfathomed councils our weakest heads defeat,
Our children rout your armies, our boats destroy your
    fleet,
And to complete the dire disgrace, cooped up within a
    town,
You live the scorn of all our host, the slaves of Wash-
    ington !

Great Heaven ! is this the nation whose thundering
    arms were hurled,
Through Europe, Afric, India? whose navy ruled a world?
The lustre of your former deeds, whole ages of renown,
Lost in a moment, or transferred to us and Washington !

Yet think not thirst of glory unsheaths our vengeful
    swords
To rend your bands assunder, or cast away your cords,
'T is heaven-born freedom fires us all, and strengthens
    each brave son,
From him who humbly guides the plough, to god-like
    Washington.

For this, oh could our wishes your ancient rage inspire,
Your armies should be doubled, in numbers, force, and
        fire.
Then might the glorious conflict prove which best de-
        served the boon,
America or Albion, a George or Washington !

Fired with the great idea, our Fathers' shades would rise,
To view the stern contention, the gods desert their skies;
And Wolfe, 'midst hosts of heroes, superior bending down,
Cry out with eager transport, God save great Washington !

Should George, too choice of Britons, to foreign realms
        apply,
And madly arm' half Europe, yet still we would defy
Turk, Hessian, Jew, and Infidel, or all those powers in
        one,
While Adams guards our senate, our camp great Wash-
        ington !

Should warlike weapons fail us, disdaining slavish fears,
To swords we 'll beat our ploughshares, our pruning-
        hooks to spears,
And rush, all desperate, on our foe, nor breathe till battle
        won,
Then shout, and shout America ! and conquering Wash-
        ington !

Proud France should view with terror, and haughty
    Spain revere,
While every warlike nation would court alliance here;
And George, his minions trembling round, dismounting
    from his throne
Pay homage to America and glorious Washington!

COLUMBIA.

By TIMOTHY DWIGHT.

(From Kettell's "Specimens," 1829. Written during the author's
service as an army chaplain, 1777-78.)

COLUMBIA, Columbia, to glory arise,
 The queen of the world, and the child of the skies;
Thy genius commands thee; with rapture behold,
While ages on ages thy splendor unfold,
Thy reign is the last, and the noblest of time,
Most fruitful thy soil most inviting thy clime ;
Let the crimes of the east ne'er encrimson thy name,
Be freedom, and science, and virtue thy fame.

To conquest and slaughter let Europe aspire ;
Whelm nations in blood, and wrap cities in fire ;
Thy heroes the rights of mankind shall defend,
And triumph pursue them, and glory attend,
A world is thy realm : for a world be thy laws,
Enlarged as thine empire, and just as thy cause ;
On Freedom's broad basis, that empire shall rise,
Extend with the main, and dissolve with the skies.

Fair science her gates to thy sons shall unbar,
And the east see the morn hide the beams of her star.
New bards, and new sages, unrivalled shall soar
To fame unextinguished, when time is no more;
To thee, the last refuge of virtue designed,
Shall fly from all nations the best of mankind;
Here, grateful to heaven, with transport shall bring
Their incense, more fragrant than odors of spring.

Nor less shall thy fair ones to glory ascend,
And genius and beauty in harmony blend;
The graces of form shall awake pure desire,
And the charms of the soul ever cherish the fire;
Their sweetness unmingled, their manners refined,
And virtue's bright image, instamped on the mind,
With peace and soft rapture shall teach life to glow,
And light up a smile in the aspect of woe.

Thy fleets to all regions thy power shall display,
The nations admire and the ocean obey;
Each shore to thy glory its tribute unfold,
And the east and the south yield their spices and gold.
As the day-spring unbounded, thy splendor shall flow,
And earth's little kingdoms before thee shall bow;
While the ensigns of union, in triumph unfurled,
Hush the tumult of war and give peace to the world.

Thus, as down a lone valley, with cedars o'erspread,
From war's dread confusion I pensively strayed,
The gloom from the face of fair heaven retired ;
The winds ceased to murmur ; the thunders expired ;
Perfumes as of Eden flowed sweetly along,
And a voice as of angels, enchantingly sung :
" Columbia, Columbia, to glory arise,
" The queen of the world, and the child of the skies."

TAXATION OF AMERICA.

BY PETER ST. JOHN, OF NORWALK, CONN.

[In Moore's "Songs and Ballads of the Revolution," this poem bears date as of 1765, but the references in it to Burgoyne's surrender, to Brandywine, etc., indicate a much later date. It is possible that a part of the poem was written and published about 1765, and that additions making reference to revolutionary incidents were made afterward. But, internal evidence renders even this assumption improbable, and suggests that the date Moore gives is the result of some mistake.—EDITOR.]

WHILE I relate my story,
    Americans give ear ;
Of Britain's fading glory
You presently shall hear ;
I 'll give a true relation,
Attend to what I say
Concerning the taxation
Of North America.

The cruel lords of Britain,
Who glory in their shame,
The project they have hit on
They joyfully proclaim ;
'T is what they 're striving after
Our right to take away,
And rob us of our charter
In North America.

There are two mighty speakers,
Who rule in Parliament,
Who ever have been seeking
Some mischief to invent ;
'T was North, and Bute his father,
The horrid plan did lay
A mighty tax to gather
In North America.

They searched the gloomy regions
Of the infernal pit,
To find among their legions
One who excelled in wit ;
To ask of him assistance,
Or tell them how they may
Subdue without resistance
This North America.

Old Satan the arch-traitor,
Who rules the burning lake,

Where his chief navigator,
Resolved a voyage to take ;
For the Britannic ocean
He launches far away,
To land he had no notion
In North America.

He takes his seat in Britain,
It was his soul's intent
Great George's throne to sit on,
And rule the Parliament ;
His comrades were pursuing
A diabolic way,
For to complete the ruin
Of North America.

He tried the art of magic
To bring his schemes about,
At length the gloomy project
He artfully found out ;
The plan was long indulgèd
In a clandestine way,
But lately was divulgèd
In North America.

These subtle arch-combiners
Addressed the British court,
All three were undersigners
Of this obscure report—

There is a pleasant landscape
That lieth far away
Beyond the wide Atlantic,
In North America.

There is a wealthy people,
Who sojourn in that land,
Their churches all with steeples
Most delicately stand :
Their houses like the gilly,
Are painted red and gay :
They flourish like the lily
In North America.

Their land with milk and honey
Continually doth flow,
The want of food or money
They seldom ever know :
They heap up golden treasure,
They have no debts to pay,
They spend their time in pleasure
In North America.

On turkeys, fowls, and fishes,
Most frequently they dine,
With gold and silver dishes
Their tables always shine.
They crown their feasts with butter,
They eat, and rise to play ;

In silks their ladies flutter,
In North America.

With gold and silver laces
They do themselves adorn,
The rubies deck their faces,
Refulgent as the morn :
Wine sparkles in their glasses,
They spend each happy day
In merriment and dances
In North America.

Let not our suit affront you,
When we address your throne ;
O King, this wealthy country
And subjects are your own,
And you, their rightful sovereign,
They truly must obey,
You have a right to govern
This North America.

O King, you 've heard the sequel
Of what we now subscribe :
Is it not just and equal
To tax this wealthy tribe ?
The question being askèd,
His majesty did say,
My subjects shall be taxèd
In North America.

Invested with a warrant,
My publicans shall go,
The tenth of all their current
They surely shall bestow;
If they indulge rebellion,
Or from my precepts stray,
I'll send my war battalion
To North America.

I'll rally all my forces
By water and by land,
My light dragoons and horses
Shall go at my command;
I'll burn both town and city,
With smoke becloud the day,
I'll show no human pity
For North America.

Go on, my hearty soldiers,
You need not fear of ill—
There's Hutchinson and Rogers,
Their functions will fulfil—
They tell such ample stories,
Believe them sure we may,
One half of them are tories
In North America.

My gallant ships are ready
To waft you o'er the flood,

And in my cause be steady,
Which is supremely good.
Go ravage, steal, and plunder,
And you shall have the prey;
They quickly will knock under
In North America.

The laws I have enacted
I never will revoke,
Although they are neglected,
My fury to provoke.
I will forbear to flatter,
I 'll rule the mighty sway,
I 'll take away the charter
From North America.

O George! you are distracted,
You 'll by experience find
The laws you have enacted
Are of the blackest kind.
I 'll make a short digression,
And tell you by the way,
We fear not your oppression
In North America.

Our fathers were distressèd
While in their native land;
By tyrants were oppressèd
As we do understand;

For freedom and religion
They were resolved to stray,
And trace the desert regions
Of North America.

Heaven was their sole protector
While on the roaring tide,
Kind fortune their director,
And providence their guide.
If I am not mistaken,
About the first of May,
This voyage was undertaken
For North America.

If rightly I remember,
This country to explore,
They landed in November
On Plymouth's desert shore.
The savages were nettled,
With fear they fled away,
So peaceably they settled
In North America.

We are their bold descendants,
For liberty we 'll fight,
The claim to independence
We challenge as our right ;
'T is what kind Heaven gave us,
Who can take it away ?

O Heaven, sure it will save us
In North America.

We never will knock under,
O George ! we do not fear
The rattling of your thunder,
Nor lightning of your spear ;
Though rebels you declare us,
We 're strangers to dismay ;
Therefore you cannot scare us
In North America.

To what you have commanded
We never will consent,
Although your troops are landed
Upon our continent ;
We 'll take our swords and muskets,
And march in dread array,
And drive the British red-coats
From North America.

We have a bold commander,
Who fears not sword or gun,
The second Alexander,
His name is Washington.
His men are all collected,
And ready for the fray,
To fight they are directed
For North America.

We 've Greene, and Gates, and Putnam,
To manage in the field,
A gallant train of footmen,
Who 'd rather die than yield;
A stately troop of horsemen
Trained in a martial way,
For to augment our forces
In North America.

Proud George, you are engagèd
All in a dirty cause,
A cruel war have wagèd
Repugnant to all laws.
Go tell the savage nations
You 're crueler than they,
To fight your own relations
In North America.

Ten millions you 've expended,
And twice ten millions more;
Our riches you intended
Should pay the mighty score.
Who now will stand your sponsor,
Your charges to defray?
For sure you cannot conquer
This North America.

I 'll tell you, George, in metre,
If you 'll attend awhile;

We 've forced your bold Sir Peter
From Sullivan's fair isle.
At Monmouth, too, we gainèd
The honors of the day—
The victory we obtainèd
For North America.

Surely we were your betters
Hard by the Brandywine ;
We laid him fast in fetters
Whose name was John Burgoyne ;
We made your Howe to tremble
With terror and dismay ;
True heroes we resemble,
In North America.

Confusion to the tories,
That black infernal name
In which Great Britain glories,
Forever to her shame ;
We 'll send each foul revolter
To smutty Africa,
Or noose him in a halter
In North America.

A health to our brave footmen,
Who handle sword and gun,
To Greene, and Gates, and Putnam,
And conquering Washington ;
Their names be wrote in letters
Which never will decay,

While sun and moon do glitter
On North America.

Success unto our allies
In Holland, France, and Spain,
Who man their ships and galleys,
Our freedom to maintain ;
May they subdue the rangers
Of proud Britannia,
And drive them from their anchors
In North America.

Success unto the Congress
Of these United States,
Who glory in the conquests
Of Washington and Gates ;
To all, both land and seamen,
Who glory in the day
When we shall all be freemen
In North America.

Success to legislation,
That rules with gentle hand,
To trade and navigation
By water and by land.
May all with one opinion
Our wholesome laws obey,
Throughout this vast dominion
Of North America.

THE BATTLE OF THE KEGS.

BY FRANCIS HOPKINSON.

(From "The Miscellaneous Essays and Occasional Writings," 1792.)

[This ballad was occasioned by a real incident. Certain machines in the form of kegs, charged with gunpowder, were sent down the river to annoy the British shipping then at Philadelphia. The danger of these machines being discovered, the British manned the wharfs and shipping, and discharged their small-arms and cannons at every thing they saw floating in the river during the ebb tide.—AUTHOR'S NOTE.]

GALLANTS attend and hear a friend
 Trill forth harmonious ditty,
Strange things I 'll tell which late befell
 In Philadelphia city.

'T was early day, as poets say,
 Just when the sun was rising,
A soldier stood on a log of wood,
 And saw a thing surprising.

72

As in amaze he stood to gaze,
  The truth can't be denied, sir,
He spied a score of kegs or more
  Come floating down the tide, sir.

A sailor, too, in jerkin blue,
  This strange appearance viewing,
First damned his eyes, in great surprise,
  Then said : " Some mischief 's brewing.

" These kegs, I 'm told, the rebels hold,
  Packed up like pickled herring ;
And they 're come down to attack the town,
  In this new way of ferrying."

The soldier flew, the sailor too,
  And scared almost to death, sir,
Wore out their shoes, to spread the news,
  And ran till out of breath, sir.

Now up and down throughout the town,
  Most frantic scenes were acted ;
And some ran here, and others there,
  Like men almost distracted.

Some fire cried, which some denied,
  But said the earth had quakèd ;
And girls and boys, with hideous noise,
  Ran through the streets half nakèd.

Sir William he, snug as a flea,
　　Lay all this time a snoring,
Nor dreamed of harm as he lay warm,
　　*　　*　　*　　*　　*

Now in a fright, he starts upright,
　　Awaked by such a clatter ;
He rubs both eyes, and boldly cries :
　　For God's sake, what 's the matter ? "

At his bedside he then espied,
　　Sir Erskine at command, sir,
Upon one foot he had one boot,
　　And th' other in his hand, sir.

" Arise, arise," Sir Erskine cries,
　　" The rebels—more 's the pity,
Without a boat are afloat,
　　And ranged before the city.

" The motley crew, in vessels new,
　　With Satan for their guide, sir,
Packed up in bags, or wooden kegs,
　　Come driving down the tide, sir.

" Therefore prepare for bloody war,
　　These kegs must all be routed
Or surely we despised shall be,
　　And British courage doubted."

The royal band now ready stand
  All ranged in dread array, sir,
With stomach stout to see it out,
  And make a bloody day, sir.

The cannons roar from shore to shore,
  The small arms make a rattle;
Since wars began I 'm sure no man
  E'er saw so strange a battle.

The rebel dales, the rebel vales
  With rebel trees surrounded,
The distant woods, the hills and floods,
  With rebel echoes sounded.

The fish below swam to and fro,
  Attacked from every quarter;
Why sure, thought they, the devil 's to pay,
  'Mongst folks above the water.

The kegs, 't is said, though strongly made,
  Of rebel staves and hoops, sir,
Could not oppose their powerful foes,
  The conquering British troops, sir,

From morn to night these men of might
  Displayed amazing courage;
And when the sun was fairly down,
  Retired to sup their porridge.

A hundred men with each a pen,
 Or more upon my word, sir,
It is most true would be too few,
 Their valor to record, sir.

Such feats did they perform that day,
 Against these wicked kegs, sir,
That years to come, if they get home,
 They 'll make their boasts and brags, sir.

CARMEN BELLICOSUM.

BY GUY HUMPHREY McMASTER.

IN their ragged regimentals
    Stood the old Continentals,
        Yielding not,
When the grenadiers were lunging,
And like hail fell the plunging
        Cannon shot ;
        When the files
        Of the isles
From the smoky night-encampment bore the banner of
    the rampant
        Unicorn,
And grummer, grummer, grummer rolled the roll of the
    drummer,
        Through the morn !

Then with eyes to the front all,
And with guns horizontal
        Stood our sires ;
And the balls whistled deadly,
And in streams flashing redly

Blazed the fires ;
As the roar
On the shore,
Swept the strong battle breakers o'er the green sodded
acres
Of the plain ;
And louder, louder, louder cracked the black gunpowder,
Cracking amain !

Now like smiths at their forges
Worked the red Saint George's
Cannoneers ;
And the " villainous saltpetre "
Rung a fierce, discordant metre
Round their ears ;
As the swift
Storm drift,
With hot, sweeping anger, came the horse guard's
clangor
On our flanks.
Then higher, higher, higher burned the old-fashioned
fire
Through the ranks !

Then the old-fashioned colonel
Galloped through the white, infernal
Powder cloud ;
And his broad sword was swinging,
And his brazen throat was ringing

Trumpet loud.
Then the blue
Bullets flew
And the trooper jackets redden at the touch of the leaden
Rifle breath ;
And rounder, rounder, rounder roared the iron six-
pounder
Hurling death !

THE YANKEE MAN-OF-WAR.

[Descriptive of the daring bravery of Captain John Paul Jones, in his cruise in the Irish Channel in 1778.]

(From Admiral Luce's " Naval Songs.")

'TIS of a gallant Yankee ship that flew the stripes and stars,
And the whistling wind from the west-nor'-west blew through the pitch-pine spars,—
With her starboard tacks a-board, my boys, she hung upon the gale,
On an autumn night we raised the light on the old head of Kinsale.

It was a clear and cloudless night, and the wind blew
   steady and strong,
As gaily over the sparkling deep our good ship bowled
   along;
With the foaming seas beneath her bow the fiery waves
   she spread,
And bending low her bosom of snow, she buried her lee
   cat-head.

There was no talk of short'ning sail by him who walked
   the poop,
And under the press of her pond'ring jib, the boom bent
   like a hoop!
And the groaning water-ways told the strain that held
   her stout main-tack,
Bnt he only laughed as he glanced aloft at a white and
   silv'ry track.

The mid-tide meets in the channel waves that flow from
   shore to shore,
And the mist hung heavy upon the land from Feather-
   stone to Dunmore,
And that sterling light in Tusker Rock where the old
   bell tolls each hour,
And the beacon light that shone so bright was quench'd
   on Waterford Tower.

The nightly robes our good ship wore were her three top-
   sails set
Her spanker and her standing jib—the courses being fast;

"Now, lay aloft! my heroes bold, let not a moment
  pass!"
And royals and top-gallant sails were quickly on each
  mast.

What looms upon our starboard bow?   What hangs upon
  the breeze?
'T is time our good ship hauled her wind a-breast the old
  Saltee's,
For by her ponderous press of sail and by her consorts four
We saw our morning visitor was a British man-of-war.

Up spake our noble Captain then, as a shot ahead of us
  past—
"Haul snug your flowing courses! lay your topsail to the
  mast!"
Those Englishmen gave three loud hurrahs from the deck
  of their covered ark,
And we answered back by a solid broadside from the
  decks of our patriot bark.

"Out booms! out booms!" our skipper cried, "out
  booms and give her sheet,"
And the swiftest keel that was ever launched shot ahead
  of the British fleet,
And a-midst a thundering shower of shot with stun'-sails
  hoisting away,
Down the North Channel Paul Jones did steer just at the
  break of day.

PAUL JONES' VICTORY

(Battle between the *Bon Homme Richard* and the *Serapis*, September 23, 1779.)

AN American Frigate:—a frigate
of fame,
With guns mounting forty, *The
Richard* by name,
Sailed to cruise in the channels of old England,
With a valiant commander, Paul Jones was his name.
Hurrah! Hurrah! Our country forever, Hurrah!

We had not cruised long, before he espies
A large forty-four, and a twenty likewise;
Well manned with bold seamen, well laid in with stores,
In consort to drive us from old England's shores.
Hurrah! Hurrah! Our country forever, Hurrah!

About twelve at noon, Pearson came alongside,
With a loud speaking trumpet, "Whence came you?"
    he cried :
"Return me an answer—I hailed you before,
Or if you do not, a broadside I 'll pour." Hurrah !

Paul Jones then said to his men, every one,
"Let every true seaman stand firm to his gun !
We 'll receive a broadside from this bold Englishman,
And like true Yankee sailors, return it again." Hurrah !

The contest was bloody, both decks ran with gore,
And the sea seemed to blaze, while the cannon did roar.
"Fight on, my brave boys," then Paul Jones he cried,
"And soon we will humble this bold Englishman's pride."
    Hurrah !

"Stand firm to your quarters—your duty don't shun,
The first one that shrinks, through the body I 'll run,
Though their force is superior, yet they shall know,
What true, brave American seamen can do." Hurrah !

The battle rolled on, till bold Pearson cried :
"Have you yet struck your colors? then come along-
    side !"
But so far from thinking that the battle was won,
Brave Paul Jones replied : "I 've not yet begun !"
    Hurrah !

We fought them eight glasses, eight glasses so hot,
Till seventy bold seamen lay dead on the spot.
And ninety brave seamen lay stretched in their gore,
While the pieces of cannon most fiercely did roar.

Our gunner, in great fright to Captain Jones came,
" We gain water quite fast and our side 's in a flame."
Then Paul Jones said in the height of his pride :
" If we cannot do better, boys, sink alongside ! "

The *Alliance* bore down, and the *Richard* did rake,
Which caused the bold hearts of our seamen to ache :
Our shots flew so hot that they could not stand us long,
And the undaunted Union-of-Britain came down.

To us they did strike and their colors hauled down ;
The fame of Paul Jones to the world shall be known,
His name shall rank with the gallant and brave,
Who fought like a hero—our freedom to save.

Now all valiant seamen where'er you may be,
Who hear of this combat that 's fought on the sea,
May you all do like them, when called to do the same,
And your names be enrolled on the pages of fame.

Your country will boast of her sons that are brave,
And to you she will look from all dangers to save,
She 'll call you dear sons, in her anuals you 'll shine,
And the brows of the brave shall green laurels entwine.

So now, my brave boys, have we taken a prize—
A large 44, and a 20 likewise !
Then God bless the mother whose doom is to weep
The loss of her sons in the ocean so deep.

1813.

THE ROYAL ADVENTURER.

BY PHILIP FRENEAU.

[In the year 1781, Prince William Henry (afterward William IV.), third son of George III., came to New York as a midshipman, accompanied by Admiral Digby. The tory authorities of the city overwhelmed the boy— he was just sixteen years old—with adulation, recording it as their conviction that his gracious presence in the country would shame the patriots out of their rebellion and win them to submission and loyalty.—EDITOR.]

PRINCE WILLIAM, of the Brunswick race,
　　To witness George's sad disgrace
　The royal lad came over,
Rebels to kill, by right divine—
Derived from that illustrious line,
　The beggars of Hanover.

So many chiefs got broken pates
In vanquishing the rebel states,
  So many nobles fell,
That George the Third in passion cried :
" Our royal blood must now be tried ;
  'T is that must break the spell ;

" To you [the fat pot-valiant swain
To Digby said], dear friend of mine,
  To you I trust my boy ;
The rebel tribes shall quake with fears,
Rebellion die when he appears,
  My tories leap with joy."

So said, so done—the lad was sent,
But never reached the continent,
  An island held him fast—
Yet there his friends danced rigadoons,
The Hessians sung in high Dutch tunes,
  " Prince William 's come at last !"

"Prince William 's come !"—the Briton cried—
" Our labors now will be repaid—
  Dominion be restored—
Our monarch is in William seen,
He is the image of our queen,
  Let William be adored !"

The tories came with long address,
With poems groaned the royal press,
　And all in William's praise—
The youth, astonished, looked about
To find their vast dominions out,
　Then answered in amaze :

" Where all your vast domain can be,
Friends, for my soul I cannot see ;
　'T is but an empty name ;
Three wasted islands and a town
　In rubbish buried—half burnt down,
　Is all that we can claim ;

" I am of royal birth, 't is true,
But what, my sons, can princes do,
　No armies to command ?
Cornwallis conquered and distrest—
Sir Henry Clinton grown a jest—
　I curse—and quit the land."

EUTAW SPRINGS.

TO THE MEMORY OF THE BRAVE AMERICANS, UNDER
GENERAL GREENE, IN SOUTH CAROLINA, WHO FELL
IN THE ACTION OF SEPTEMBER 8, 1781, AT EUTAW
SPRINGS.

BY PHILIP FRENEAU.

AT Eutaw Springs the valiant died :
    Their limbs with dust are covered o'er—
Weep on, ye springs, your tearful tide ;
    How many heroes are no more !

If in this wreck of ruin they
    Can yet be thought to claim a tear,
O smite thy gentle breast, and say
    The friends of freedom slumber here !

Thou who shalt trace this bloody plain,
    If goodness rules thy generous breast,
Sigh for the wasted, rural reign ;
    Sigh for the shepherds, sunk to rest !

Stranger, their humble graves adorn ;
　　You too may fall and ask a tear ;
'T is not the beauty of the morn
　　That proves the evening shall be clear—

They saw their injured country's woe;
　　The flaming town, the wasted field ;
Then rushed to meet the insulting foe ;
　　They took the spear,—but left the shield.

Led by thy conquering genius, Greene,
　　The Britons they compelled to fly ;
None distant viewed the fatal plain,
　　None grieved, in such a cause to die—

But, like the Parthian, famed of old,
　　Who, flying still their arrows threw;
These routed Britons, full as bold,
　　Retreated, and retreating slew.

Now rest in peace, our patriot band ;
　　Though far from Nature's limits thrown,
We trust they find a happier land,
　　A brighter sunshine of their own.

AN ANCIENT PROPHECY.

By PHILIP FRENEAU.

(Written soon after the surrender of Cornwallis.)

WHEN a certain great King, whose initial is G.,
    Forces stamps upon paper and folks to drink tea;
When these folks burn his tea and stampt-paper, like
    stubble,
You may guess that this King is then coming to trouble.

But when a Petition he treads under feet,
And sends over the ocean an army and fleet,
When that army, half famished, and frantic with rage,
Is cooped up with a leader whose name rhymes to *cage;*
When that leader goes home, dejected and sad;
You may then be assur'd the King's prospects are bad.

But when B. and C. with their armies are taken
This King will do well if he saves his own bacon:
In the year Seventeen hundred and eighty and two
A stroke he shall get, that will make him look blue;

And soon, very soon, shall the season arrive,
When Nebuchadnezzar to pasture shall drive.

In the year eighty-three, the affair will be over
And he shall eat turnips that grow in Hanover ;
The face of the Lion will then become pale,
He shall yield fifteen teeth and be sheared of his tail—
O King, my dear King, you shall be very sore,
From the *Stars* and the *Stripes* you will mercy implore,
And your Lion shall growl, but hardly bite more.—

THE DANCE.

(Published soon after the surrender of Cornwallis.)

CORNWALLIS led a country dance,
　The like was never seen, sir,
Much retrogade and much advance,
　And all with General Greene, sir.

They rambled up and rambled down,
　Joined hands, then off they run, sir.
Our General Greene to Charlestown,
　The earl to Wilmington, sir.

Greene in the South then danced a set,
　And got a mighty name, sir,
Cornwallis jigged with young Fayette,
　But suffered in his fame, sir.

Then down he figured to the shore,
　Most like a lordly dancer,
And on his courtly honor swore
　He would no more advance, sir.

Quoth he, my guards are weary grown
   With footing country dances,
They never at St. James's shone,
   At capers, kicks or prances.

Though men so gallant ne'er were seen,
   While sauntering on parade, sir,
Or wriggling o'er the park's smooth green,
   Or at a masquerade, sir.

Yet are red heels and long-laced skirts,
   For stumps and briars meet, sir?
Or stand they chance with hunting-shirts,
   Or hardy veteran feet, sir?

Now housed in York, he challenged all,
   At minuet or all 'amande,
And lessons for a courtly ball
   His guards by day and night conned.

This challenge known, full soon there came,
   A set who had the bon ton,
De Grasse and Rochambeau, whose fame
   Fut brillant pour un long tems.

And Washington, Columbia's son,
   Whom easy nature taught, sir,
That grace which can't by pains be won,
   Or Plutus's gold be bought, sir.

Now hand in hand they circle round
    This ever-dancing peer, sir ;
Their gentle movements soon confound
    The earl as they draw near, sir.

His music soon forgets to play—
    His feet can move no more,* sir,
And all his bands now curse the day
    They jiggèd to our shore, sir.

Now Tories all, what can ye say?
    Come—is not this a griper,
That while your hopes are danced away,
    'T is you must pay the piper?

1781.

---

* In all the versions of this poem examined by the editor this line reads " His feet can no more move, sir " ; but the reading is so clearly wrong that it seems proper to amend it so that the obviously intended rhyme between " more, sir " and " shore, sir " shall appear. There is the greater justification for the taking of this liberty of correction because the poem originally appeared in carelessly edited contemporary prints.—EDITOR.

SONG OF MARION'S MEN.

By WILLIAM CULLEN BRYANT.

[A very interesting bit of literary history attaches to this poem. The piece appeared in Mr. Bryant's first collected volume of poems about 1831. Mr. Bryant sent the volume, with a letter, to Washington Irving, then in London, with whom he had no personal acquaintance, and invoked his good offices in inducing Murray to bring out an English edition of the work. The time being peculiarly unpropitious, Murray declined to undertake the venture, but Irving found another publisher, and himself introduced the volume in the most favorable manner, with a dedicatory letter of his own. While passing the book through the press the publisher observed in this poem the lines:

> " The British soldier trembles
> When Marion's name is told,"

and assured Irving that he could not offer a work con-
taining such a statement to a British public. It was im-
possible to consult the author, three thousand miles away,
and Irving ventured to change the objectionable passage
so that it should read :

> " The foeman trembles in his camp
> When Marion's name is told."

There is no reason to believe that Mr. Bryant ever re-
sented the liberty or regarded it otherwise than as an act
of friendly intervention ; but some years later William
Leggett, who had long been Mr. Bryant's editorial asso-
ciate in the office of the *Evening Post*, but had severed
his connection with that paper, made a virulent assault
upon Irving in the *Plaindealer* on account of the change
he had made, even going so far as to intimate that both
that and his dealings with one of his own works were
dictated by mean sycophancy and cowardice on Irving's
part.—EDITOR.]

SONG OF MARION'S MEN.

OUR band is few, but true and tried,
   Our leader frank and bold ;
The British soldier trembles
   When Marion's name is told.
Our fortress is the good greenwood,
   Our tent the cypress tree ;
We know the forest round us ;
   As seamen know the sea ;
We know its walls of thorny vines,
   Its glades of reedy grass,
Its safe and silent islands
   Within the dark morass.

99

Woe to the English soldiery
  That little dread us near !
On them shall light at midnight
  A strange and sudden fear ;
When, waking to their tents on fire,
  They grasp their arms in vain,
And they who stand to face us
  Are beat to earth again ;
And they who fly in terror deem
  A mighty host behind,
And hear the tramp of thousands
  Upon the hollow wind.

Then sweet the hour that brings release
  From danger and from toil ;
We talk the battle over,
  And share the battle's spoil.
The woodland rings with laugh and shout,
  As if a hunt were up,
And woodland flowers are gathered
  To crown the soldier's cup.
With merry songs we mock the wind
  That in the pine-top grieves,
And slumber long and sweetly
  On beds of oaken leaves.

Well knows the fair and friendly moon
  The band that Marion leads,—

The glitter of their rifles,
  The scampering of their steeds.
'T is life to guide the fiery barb
  Across the moonlight plain ;
'T is life to feel the night wind
  That lifts his tossing mane.
A moment in the British camp—
  A moment—and away
Back to the pathless forest,
  Before the peep of day.

Grave men there are by broad Santee,
  Grave men with hoary hairs ;
Their hearts are all with Marion,
  For Marion are their prayers.
And lovely ladies greet our band
  With kindliest welcoming,
With smiles like those of summer,
  And tears like those of spring.
For them we wear these trusty arms,
  And lay them down no more
Till we have driven the Briton
  Forever from our shore.

HAIL, COLUMBIA.

BY JOSEPH HOPKINSON.

(First sung at the Chestnut Street Theatre, Philadelphia, in 1798.)

[This song was inspired by the troubles with France, which threatened but did not actually result in open war. For convenience it is classed with the ballads and lyrics of the Revolution, to the actors in which its references point, though, strictly speaking, it belongs to none of the groups into which this collection is divided.— EDITOR.]

HAIL ! Columbia, happy land !
    Hail ! ye heroes, heav'n-born band,
Who fought and bled in freedom's cause,
Who fought and bled in freedom's cause,
And when the storm of war was gone,
Enjoyed the peace your valor won ;
Let independence be your boast,
Ever mindful what it cost,

Ever grateful for the prize,
Let its altar reach the skies.

Chorus.

Firm, united let us be,
Rallying round our liberty,
As a band of brothers joined,
Peace and safety we shall find.

Immortal patriots, rise once more!
Defend your rights, defend your shore;
Let no rude foe with impious hand,
Let no rude foe with impious hand
Invade the shrine where sacred lies
Of toil and blood the well-earned prize;
While offering peace, sincere and just,
In heav'n we place a manly trust,
That truth and justice may prevail,
And ev'ry scheme of bondage fail.—*Chorus.*

Sound, sound the trump of fame!
Let Washington's great name
Ring thro' the world with loud applause!
Ring thro' the world with loud applause!
Let ev'ry clime to freedom dear
Listen with a joyful ear;
With equal skill, with steady pow'r,
He governs in the fearful hour

Of horrid war, or guides with ease
The happier time of honest peace.—*Chorus.*

Behold the chief, who now commands,
Once more to serve his country stands,
The rock on which the storm will beat!
The rock on which the storm will beat!
But armed in virtue, firm and true,
His hopes are fixed on heav'n and you.
When hope was sinking in dismay,
When gloom obscured Columbia's day,
His steady mind, from changes free,
Resolved on death or liberty.—*Chorus.*

TRUXTON'S VICTORY

(Action between the *Constellation* and the *Insurgente*, 9 Feb., 1799.)

[This song and the one that follows it relate to a naval conflict of 1799, during the troubles which for a time threatened war, between France and the United States. As the second of the two songs was written in 1813, and both were much sung at that period, it has been thought best to present both of them where one properly belongs, namely, among the poems of the last war with Great Britain.—EDITOR.]

WHEN Freedom, fair Freedom, her banner display'd,
    Defying each foe whom her rights would invade,
Columbia's brave sons swore those rights to maintain,
And o'er ocean and earth to establish her reign ;
      United they cry,
      While that standard shall fly,

Resolved, firm, and steady,
We always are ready
To fight, and to conquer, to conquer or die.

Tho' Gallia through Europe has rushed like a flood,
And deluged the earth with an ocean of blood :
While by faction she 's led, while she 's governed by
　　knaves,
We court not her smiles, and will ne'er be her slaves ;
　　　　Her threats we defy,
　　　　While our standard shall fly,
　　　　Resolved, firm, and steady,
　　　　We always are ready
To fight, and to conquer, to conquer or die.

Tho' France with caprice dares our Statesmen upbraid,
A tribute demands, or sets bounds to our trade ;
From our young rising Navy our thunders shall roar,
And our Commerce extend to the earth's utmost shore.
　　　　Our cannon we 'll ply,
　　　　While our standard shall fly ;
　　　　Resolved, firm, and steady,
　　　　We always are ready
To fight, and to conquer, to conquer or die.

To know we 're resolved, let them think on the hour,
When Truxton, brave Truxton off Nevis's shore,
His ship mann'd for battle, the standard unfurl'd,
And at the *Insurgente* defiance he hurled ;

And his valiant tars cry,
While our standard shall fly,
Resolved, firm, and steady,
We always are ready
To fight, and to conquer, to conquer or die.

Each heart beat exulting, inspir'd by the cause ;
They fought for their country, their freedom and laws ;
From their cannon loud volleys of vengeance they pour'd,
And the standard of France to Columbia was lower'd.
Huzza ! they now cry,
Let the Eagle wave high ;
Resolved, firm, and steady,
We always are ready
To fight, and to conquer, to conquer or die.

Then raise high the strain, pay the tribute that 's due
To the fair *Constellation*, and all her brave Crew ;
Be Truxton revered, and his name be enrolled,
'Mongst the chiefs of the ocean, the heroes of old.
Each invader defy,
While such heroes are nigh,
Who always are ready,
Resolved, firm, and steady
To fight, and to conquer, to conquer or die.

THE "CONSTELLATION" AND THE "INSURGENTE."

(Action of 9 February, 1799.)

COME all ye Yankee sailors, with swords and pikes
    advance,
'T is time to try your courage and humble haughty
    France,
    The sons of France our seas invade,
    Destroy our commerce and our trade,
    'T is time the reck'ning should be paid !
        To brave Yankee boys.

On board the *Constellation*, from Baltimore we came,
We had a bold commander and Truxton was his name !
    Our ship she mounted forty guns,
    And on the main so swiftly runs,
    To prove to France Columbia's sons
        Are brave Yankee boys.

We sailed to the West Indies in order to annoy
The invaders of our commerce, to burn, sink, and destroy;

Our *Constellation* shone so bright,
The Frenchmen could not bear the sight,
And away they scamper'd in affright,
    From the brave Yankee boys.

'T was on the 9th of February, at Montserrat we lay,
And there we spy'd the *Insurgente* just at the break of
    day,
    We raised the orange and the blue,
    To see if they our signals knew,
    The *Constellation* and her crew
        Of brave Yankee boys.

Then all hands were called to quarters, while we pursued
    in chase,
With well prim'd guns, our tompions out, well spliced the
    main brace.
    Soon to the French we did draw nigh,
    Compelled to fight, they were, or fly,
    The word was passed, "CONQUER OR DIE,"
        My brave Yankee boys.

Lord! our Cannons thunder'd with peals tremendous roar,
And death upon our bullets' wings that drenched their
    decks with gore,
    The blood did from their scuppers run,
    Their chief exclaimed, "We are undone!"
    Their flag they struck, the battle won,
        By the brave Yankee boys.

Then to St. Kitts we steered, we bro't her safe in port,
The grand salute was fired and answered from the fort,
    John Adams in full bumpers toast,
    George Washington, Columbia's boast,
    And now "the girl we love the most!"
      My brave Yankee boys.

1813.

THE WASP'S FROLIC.

(Action of 18 October, 1812.)

[From " Naval Songster," 1815.]

'TWAS on board the sloop-of-war *Wasp* boys,
    We set sail from Delaware Bay,
To cruise on Columbia's fair coast, sirs,
    Our rights to maintain on the sea.

Three days were not passed on our station,
    When the *Frolic* came up to our view ;
Says Jones, " Show the flag of our nation " ;
    Three cheers were then gave by our crew.

We boldly bore up to this Briton,
    Whose cannon began for to roar ;
The *Wasp* soon her stings from her side ran,
    When we on them a broadside did pour.

Each sailor stood firm at his quarters,
    'T was minutes past forty and three,
When fifty bold Britons were slaughter'd,
    Whilst our guns swept their masts in the sea.

Their breasts then with valor still glowing,
    Acknowledged the battle we 'd won,
On us then bright laurels bestowing,
    When to leeward they fired a gun.

On their decks we the twenty guns counted,
    With a crew for to answer the same ;
Eighteen was the number we mounted,
    Being served by the lads of true game.

With the *Frolic* in tow, we were standing,
    All in for Columbia's fair shore ;
But fate on our laurels was frowning,
    We were taken by a seventy-four.

"CONSTITUTION" AND "GUERRIÈRE."

(Action of 19 August, 1812.)

IT oft times has been told,
 That the British seamen bold,
Could flog the tars of France so neat and handy, oh !
 But they never found their match,
 Till the Yankees did them catch,
Oh, the Yankee boys for fighting are the dandy, oh !

 The *Guerrière* a frigate bold,
 On the foaming ocean rolled,
Commanded by proud Dacres, the grandee, oh !

With as choice a British crew,
As a rammer ever drew,
Could flog the Frenchmen two to one so handy, oh !

When this frigate hove in view,
Says proud Dacres to his crew,
" Come clear ship for action and be handy, oh !
To the weather gage, boys, get her,"
And to make his men fight better,
Gave them to drink gun-powder mixed with brandy, oh !

Then Dacres loudly cries,
" Make this Yankee ship your prize,
You can in thirty minutes, neat and handy, oh !
Twenty-five 's enough I 'm sure,
And if you 'll do it in a score,
I 'll treat you to a double share of brandy, oh ! "

The British shot flew hot,
Which the Yankees answered not,
Till they got within the distance they called handy, oh !
" Now," says Hull unto his crew,
" Boys, let 's see what we can do,
If we take this boasting Briton we 're the dandy, oh ! "

The first broadside we pour'd
Carried her mainmast by the board,
Which made this loftly frigate look abandon'd, oh !

Then Dacres shook his head,
And to his officers said,
" Lord . I did n't think those Yankees were so handy, oh !"

Our second told so well
That their fore and mizzen fell,
Which dous'd the Royal ensign neat and handy, oh !
" By George ! " says he, " we 're done,"
And they fired a lee gun,
While the Yankees struck up Yankee Doodle Dandy, oh !

Then Dacres came on board,
To deliver up his sword,
Tho' loth was he to part with it, it was so handy, oh !
" Oh keep your sword," says Hull,
" For it only makes you dull,
" Cheer up and take a little drink of brandy, oh ! "

Now, fill your glasses full,
And we 'll drink to Captain Hull,
And so merrily we 'll push about the brandy, oh !
John Bull may toast his fill,
But let the world say what they will,
The Yankee boys for fighting are the dandy, oh !

THE "UNITED STATES" AND "MACEDONIAN."

(Action 25 of October, 1812.)

HOW glows each patriot bosom that boasts a Yankee
    heart,
To emulate such glorious deeds and nobly take a part;
    When sailors with their thund'ring guns,
    Prove to the English, French, and Danes
    That Neptune's chosen fav'rite sons
      Are brave Yankees boys.

The twenty-fifth of October, that glorious happy day,
When we beyond all precedent, from Britons bore the
    sway,—
    'T was in the ship *United States*,
    Four and forty guns the rates,
    That she should rule, decreed the Fates,
      And brave Yankee boys,

Decatur and his hardy tars were cruising on the deep,
When off the Western Islands they to and fro did sweep,
    The *Macedonian* they espied,

118

"Huzza ! bravo !" Decatur cried,
"We 'll humble Britain's boasted pride,
　　My brave Yankee boys."

The decks were cleared, the hammocks stowed, the boat-
　　swain pipes all hands,
The tompions out, the guns well sponged, the Captain now
　　commands ;
　　The boys who for their country fight,
　　Their words, "Free Trade and Sailor's Rights !"
　　Three times they cheered with all their might,
　　　　Those brave Yankee boys.

Now chain-shot, grape, and langrage pierce through her
　　oaken sides,
And many a gallant sailor's blood runs purpling in the
　　tides ;
　　While death flew nimbly o'er their decks,
　　Some lost their legs, and some their necks,
　　And Glory's wreath our ship be-decks,
　　　　For brave Yankee boys.

My boys, the proud St. George's Cross, the stripes above
　　it wave,
And busy are our gen'rous tars, the conquered foe to save,
　　Our Captain cries "Give me your hand,"
　　Then of the ship who took command
　　　　But brave Yankee boys ?

Our enemy lost her mizzen, her main and fore-top-mast,
For ev'ry shot with death was winged, which slew her
    men so fast,
      That they lost five to one in killed,
      And ten to one their blood was spilled,
      So Fate decreed and Heaven had willed,
        For brave Yankee boys.

Then homeward steered the captive ship, now safe in
    port she lies,
The old and young with rapture viewed our sailors'
    noble prize ;
      Through seas of wine their health we 'll drink,
      And wish them sweet-hearts, friends, and chink,
      Who 'fore they 'd strike, will nobly sink
        Our brave Yankee boys.

    1813.

THE "UNITED STATES" AND "MACEDONIAN."

(Action of 25 October, 1812.)

THE banner of Freedom high floated unfurled,
  While the silver-tipt surges in low homage curled,
Flashing bright round the bow of Decatur's brave bark,
In contest, an "eagle "—in chasing a "lark."
      The bold *United States*,
      Which four-and-forty rates,
Will ne'er be known to yield—be known to yield or fly,
Her motto is "Glory ! we conquer or we die."

All canvas expanded to woo the coy gale,
The ship cleared for action, in chase of a sail ;
The foemen in view, every bosom beats high,
All eager for conquest, or ready to die.
      The bold *United States*,
      Which four-and-forty rates,
Will ne'er be known to yield—be known to yield or fly.
Her motto is "Glory ! we conquer or we die."

Now havoc stands ready, with optics of flame,
And battle-hounds "strain on the start" for the game ;
The blood demons rise on the surge for their prey,
While Pity, rejected, awaits the dread fray.

        The bold *United States*,
        Which four-and-forty rates,
Will ne'er be known to yield—be known to yield or fly,
Her motto is " Glory ! we conquer or we die."

The gay floating streamers of Britain appear,
Waving light on the breeze as the stranger we near ;
And now could the quick-sighted Yankee discern
" *Macedonian*," emblazoned at large on her stern.

        The bold *United States*,
        Which four-and-forty rates,
Will ne'er be known to yield—be known to yield or fly,
Her motto is " Glory ! we conquer or we die."

She waited our approach, and the contest began,
But to waste ammunition is no Yankee plan ;
In awful suspense every match was withheld,
While the bull-dogs of Britain incessantly yelled.

        The bold *United States*,
        Which four-and-forty rates,
Will ne'er be known to yield—be known to yield or fly,
Her motto is " Glory ! we conquer or we die."

Unawed by her thunders, alongside we came,
While the foe seemed enwrapped in a mantle of flame;
When, prompt to the word, such a flood we return,
That Neptune aghast, thought his trident would burn.
   The bold *United States*,
    Which four-and-forty rates,
Will ne'er be known to yield—be known to yield or fly,
Her motto is " Glory ! we conquer or we die."

Now the lightning of battle gleams horridly red,
With a tempest of iron and hail-storm of lead;
And our fire on the foe we so copiously poured,
His mizzen and topmasts soon went by the board.
   The bold *United States*,
    Which four-and-forty rates,
Will ne'er be known to yield—be known to yield or fly,
Her motto is " Glory ! we conquer or we die."

So fierce and so bright did our flashes aspire,
They thought that their cannon had set us on fire,
" The Yankee 's in flames !—every British tar hears,
And hails the false omen with three hearty cheers.
   The bold *United States*,
    Which four-and-forty rates,
Will ne'er be known to yield—be known to yield or fly,
Her motto is " Glory ! we conquer or we die."

In seventeen minutes they found their mistake,
And were glad to surrender and fall in our wake;
Her decks were with carnage and blood deluged o'er,
Where welt'ring in blood lay an hundred and four.
       The bold *United States*,
         Which four-and-forty rates,
Will ne'er be known to yield—be known to yield or fly,
Her motto is "Glory! we conquer or we die."

But though she was made so completely a wreck,
With blood they had scarcely encrimsoned our deck;
Only five valiant Yankees in the contest were slain,
And our ship in five minutes was fitted again.
       The bold *United States*,
         Which four-and-forty rates,
Will ne'er be known to yield—be known to yield or fly,
Her motto is "Glory! we conquer or we die."

Let Britain no longer lay claim to the seas,
For the trident of Neptune is ours, if we please,
While Hull and Decatur and Jones are our boast,
We dare their whole navy to come on our coast.
       The bold *United States*,
         Which four-and-forty rates,
Will ne'er be known to yield—be known to yield or fly,
Her motto is "Glory! we conquer or we die."

Rise, tars of Columbia!—and share in the fame,
Which gilds Hull's, Decatur's and Jones's bright name ;
Fill a bumper, and drink, " Here 's success to the cause,
But Decatur supremely deserves our applause."
       The bold *United States*,
       Which four-and-forty rates,
Shall ne'er be known to yield—be known to yield or fly,
Her motto is "Glory ! we conquer or we die."

1813.

PERRY'S VICTORY.

(Battle of Lake Erie, 10 September, 1813.)

[This ballad, clumsy as it is in construction, was very popular in its day, mainly, perhaps, because of the peculiarly dramatic character of the action it was written to celebrate.—EDITOR.]

WE sailed to and fro in Erie's broad lake,
    To find British bullies or get into their wake,
When we hoisted our canvas with true Yankee speed,
And the brave Captain Perry our squadron did lead.

We sailed thro' the lake, boys, in search of the foe,
In the cause of Columbia our brav'ry to show,
To be equal in combat was all our delight,
As we wished the proud Britons to know we could fight.

And whether like Yeo, boys, they 'd taken affright,
We could see not, nor find them by day or by night;
So cruising we went in a glorious cause,
In defence of our rights, our freedom, and laws.

At length to our liking six sails hove in view,
Huzzah ! says brave Perry, huzzah ! says his crew,
And then for the chase, boys, with our brave little crew,
We fell in with the bullies and gave them "burgoo."

Though the force was unequal, determined to fight,
We brought them to action before it was night ;
We let loose our thunder, our bullets did fly,
"Now give them your shot, boys," our commander did
    cry.

We gave them a broadside, our cannon to try,
"Well done," says brave Perry, " for quarter they 'll cry,
Shot well home, my brave boys, they shortly shall see,
That quite brave as they are, still braver are we."

Then we drew up our squadron, each man full of fight,
And put the proud Britons in a terrible plight,
The brave Perry's movements will prove fully as bold,
As the fam'd Admiral Nelson's prowess of old.

The conflict was sharp, boys, each man to his guns,
For our country, her glory, the vict'ry was won,
So six sail (the whole fleet) was our fortune to take,
Here 's a health to brave Perry, who governs the Lake.

1813.

YANKEE THUNDERS.

BRITANNIA'S gallant streamers,
　　Float proudly o'er the tide,
And fairly wave Columbia's stripes,
　　In battle side by side.
And ne'er did bolder seamen meet,
　　Where ocean's surges pour ;
O'er the tide now they ride,
　　While the bell'wing thunders roar,
While the cannon's fire is flashing fast,
　　And the bell'wing thunders roar.

When Yankee meets the Briton,
　　Whose blood congenial flows,
By Heav'n created to be friends,
　　By fortune rendered foes ;
Hard then must be the battle fray,
　　Ere well the fight is o'er ;
Now they ride, side by side,
　　While the bell'wing thunders roar,
While her cannon's fire is flashing fast,
　　And the bell'wing thunders roar.

Still, still, for noble England
  Bold D'Acres' streamers fly ;
And for Columbia, gallant Hull's
  As proudly and as high ;
Now louder rings the battle din,
  And thick the volumes pour ;
Still they ride, side by side,
  While the bell'wing thunders roar,
While the cannon's fire is flashing fast,
  And the bell'wing thunders roar.

Why lulls Britannia's thunder,
  That waked the wat'ry war ?
Why stays the gallant *Guerrière*,
  Whose streamers waved so fair ?
That streamer drinks the ocean wave,
  That warrior's fight is o'er !
Still they ride, side by side,
  While the bell'wing thunders roar,
While the cannon's fire is flashing fast,
  And the bell'wing thunders roar.

Hark ! 't is the Briton's lee gun !
  Ne'er bolder warrior kneeled !
And ne'er to gallant mariners
  Did braver seamen yield.
Proud be the sires, whose hardy boys
  Then fell to fight no more :

With the brave, mid the wave;
  When the cannon's thunders roar,
Their spirits then shall trim the blast,
  And swell the thunder's roar.

Vain were the cheers of Britons,
  Their hearts did vainly swell,
Where virtue, skill, and bravery
  With gallant Morris fell.
That heart so well in battle tried,
  Along the Moorish shore,
And again o'er the main,
  When Columbia's thunders roar,
Shall prove its Yankee spirit true,
  When Columbia's thunder's roar.

Hence be our floating bulwark
  Those oaks our mountains yield;
'T is mighty Heaven's plain decree—
  Then take the wat'ry field!
To ocean's farthest barrier then
  Your whit'ning sail shall pour;
Safe they 'll ride o'er the tide,
  While Columbia's thunders roar,
While her cannon's fire is flashing fast,
  And her Yankee thunders roar.

1813.

YE PARLIAMENT OF ENGLAND.

[This rudely constructed song—evidently composed in the forecastle, where poets are not exigent in the matter of rhymes, is included in this collection, notwithstanding its imperfections, because of the hold it took upon the minds of patriotic people. It was still a favorite song in many parts of the country as late as 1859, and it is valuable as a reflection of the spirit in which the War of 1812–14 was regarded by those who fought it.—EDITOR.]

YE parliament of England,
   You lords and commons, too,
Consider well what you 're about,
   And what you 're going to do ;
You 're now to fight with Yankees,
   I 'm sure you 'll rue the day,
You roused the sons of liberty,
   In North America.

You first confined our commerce,
   And said our ships shant trade,

You next impressed our seamen,
  And used them as your slaves;
You then insulted Rogers,
  While ploughing o'er the main,
And had not we declarèd war,
  You 'd have done it o'er again.

You thought our frigates were but few,
  And Yankees could not fight,
Until brave Hull your *Guerrière* took
  And banished her from your sight.
The *Wasp* then took your *Frolic*,
  We 'll nothing say to that,
The *Poictiers* being of the line,
  Of course she took her back.

The next, your *Macedonian*,
  No finer ship could swim,
Decatur took her gilt-work off,
  And then he sent her in.
The *Java*, by a Yankee ship
  Was sunk, you all must know;
The *Peacock* fine, in all her plume,
  By Lawrence down did go.

Then next you sent your *Boxer*,
  To box us all about,
But we had an *Enterprising* brig
  That beat your *Boxer* out;

We boxed her up to Portland,
  And moored her off the town,
To show the sons of liberty
  The *Boxer* of renown.

The next upon Lake Erie,
  Where Perry had some fun,
You own he beat your naval force,
  And caused them for to run;
This was to you a sore defeat,
  The like ne'er known before—
Your British squadron beat complete—
  Some took, some run ashore.

There 's Rogers in the *President*,
  Will burn, sink, and destroy;
The *Congress*, on the Brazil coast,
  Your commerce will annoy;
The *Essex*, in the South Seas,
  Will put out all your lights,
The flag she waves at her mast-head—
  " Free Trade and Sailor's Rights."

Lament, ye sons of Britain,
  Far distant is the day,
When you 'll regain by British force
  What you 've lost in America;
Go tell your king and parliament,
  By all the world 't is known,

That British force, by sea and land,
  By Yankees is o'erthrown.

Use every endeavor,
  And strive to make a peace,
For Yankee ships are building fast,
  Their navy to increase ;
They will enforce their commerce,
  The laws by heaven are made,
That Yankee ships in time of peace,
  To any port may trade.

1813.

COMRADES! JOIN THE FLAG OF GLORY.

COMRADES! join the flag of glory,
    Cheerily tread the deck of fame,
Earn a place in future story,
    Seek and win a warrior's name.

Yankee tars can laugh at dangers,
    While the roaring mountain wave
Teems with carnage—they are strangers
    To a deed that is not brave.

May our bannered stars as ever
    Splendidly o'er freemen burn,
Till the night of war is over,
    Till the dawn of peace return.

    1813.

OUR NAVY.

ON wings of glory, swift as light,
　　The sound of battle came,
The gallant Hull in glorious fight
　　Has won the wreaths of fame.

Chorus.—Let brave Columbia's noble band
　　　　With hearts united rise,
　　Swear to protect their native land
　　　　Till sacred freedom dies.

　　Let brave Decatur's dauntless breast
　　　　With patriot ardor glow,
　　And in the garb of vict'ry drest
　　　　Triumphant blast the foe.
Chorus.—Let brave, etc.

　　And Rogers with his gallant crew
　　　　O'er the wide ocean ride,
　　To prove their loyal spirits true,
　　　　And crush old Albion's pride.
Chorus.—Let brave, etc.

Then hail another *Guerrière* there,
   With roaring broadsides hail ;
And while the thunder rends the air
   See Briton's sons turn pale.
Chorus.—Let brave, etc.

   " The day is ours, my boys, huzza ! "
   The great commander cries,
While all responsive roar huzza !
   With pleasure-sparkling eyes.
Chorus.—Let brave etc.

Thus shall Columbia's fame be spread,
   Her heaven-born eagle soar ;
Her deeds of glory shall be read
   When tyrants are no more.
Chorus.—Let brave, etc.

1813.

THE STAR-SPANGLED BANNER.

BY FRANCIS SCOTT KEY.

[Written during the bombardment of Fort McHenry,
below Baltimore, by the British fleet, 1814, the author
being at the time forcibly detained on board one of
the British ships.—EDITOR.]

O SAY, can you see by the dawn's early light,
    What so proudly we hailed at the twilight's last
       gleaming?
Whose broad stripes and bright stars through the perilous
      fight,
  On the ramparts we watched were so gallantly stream-
      ing ;
And the rocket's red glare, the bombs bursting in air,
Gave proof through the night that our flag was still
      there.
  O say, does the star-spangled banner yet wave
  O'er the land of the free and the home of the brave?

On the shore dimly seen, through the mists of the deep,
  Where the foe's haughty host in dread silence reposes,
What is that which the breeze, o'er the towering steep,
  As it fitfully blows, half conceals, half discloses?
Now it catches the gleam of the morning's first beam,
In full glory reflected now shines on the stream.
  'T is the star-spangled banner! O long may it wave
  O'er the land of the free and the home of the brave!

And where is that band who so vauntingly swore
  That the havoc of war and the battle's confusion
A home and a country shall leave us no more?
  Their blood has washed out their foul footsteps' pollu-
    tion.
No refuge could save the hireling and slave,
From the terror of death and the gloom of the grave.
  And the star-spangled banner in triumph shall wave
  O'er the land of the free and the home of the brave !

O thus be it ever when freemen shall stand
  Between their loved homes and the war's desolation ;
Blest with vict'ry and peace, may the heaven-rescued
    land,
  Praise the power that has made and preserved us a na-
    tion.
Then conquer we must, for our cause it is just.
And this be our motto : "In God is our trust."
  And the star-spangled banner in triumph shall wave
  O'er the land of the free and the home of the brave.

SEA AND LAND VICTORIES.

(From " The Naval Songster," 1815.)

WITH half the Western world at stake,
    See Perry on the midland lake,
      The unequal combat dare ;
Unawed by vastly stronger pow'rs,
He met the foe and made him ours,
      And closed the savage war.

Macdonough, too, on Lake Champlain,
In ships outnumbered, guns, and men,
      Saw dangers thick increase ;
His trust in God and virtue's cause
He conquer'd in the lion's jaws,
      And led the way to peace.

To sing each valiant hero's name
Whose deeds have swelled the files of fame,
      Requires immortal powers ;

Columbia's warriors never yield
To equal force by sea or field,
  Her eagle never cowers.

Long as Niagara's cataract roars
Or Erie laves our Northern shores,
  Great Brown, thy fame shall rise ;
Outnumber'd by a veteran host
Of conquering heroes, Britain's boast—
  Conquest was there thy prize.

At Plattsburg, see the Spartan band,
Where gallant Macomb held command,
  The unequal host oppose ;
Provost confounded, vanquished flies,
Convinced that numbers won't suffice
  Where Freemen are the foes.

Our songs to noblest strains we 'll raise
While we attempt thy matchless praise,
  Carolina's godlike son ;
While Mississippi rolls his flood,
Or Freemen's hearts move patriots' blood,
  The palm shall be thine own.

At Orleans—lo ! a savage band,
In countless numbers gain the strand,
  " Beauty and spoil " the word—

There Jackson with his fearless few,
The invincibles by thousands slew,
    And dire destruction poured.

O Britain! when the tale is told
Of Jackson's deeds by fame enrolled,
    Should grief and madness rise,
Remember God, the avenger, reigns,
Who witnessed Havre's smoking plains,
    And Hampton's female cries.

OLD IRONSIDES.

BY OLIVER WENDELL HOLMES.

[This poem was inspired by the announcement that
the frigate *Constitution* was to be dismantled. Though
written later it belongs among the poems of the War of
1812, as the *Constitution's* fame was won in that war.—
EDITOR.]

A Y, tear her tattered ensign down !
    Long has it waved on high,
And many an eye has dimmed to see
    That banner in the sky ;
Beneath it rung the battle shout,
    And burst the cannon's roar ;—
The meteor of the ocean air
    Shall sweep the clouds no more.

Her deck, once red with heroes' blood,
    Where knelt the vanquished foe,
When winds were hurrying o'er the flood,
    And waves were white below,

No more shall feel the victor's tread,
  Or know the conquered knee ;—
The harpies of the shore shall pluck
  The eagle of the sea !

O better that her shattered hulk
  Should sink beneath the wave ;
Her thunders shook the mighty deep,
  And there should be her grave ;
Nail to the mast her holy flag,
  Set every threadbare sail,
And give her to the god of storms,
  The lightning and the gale !

1836.

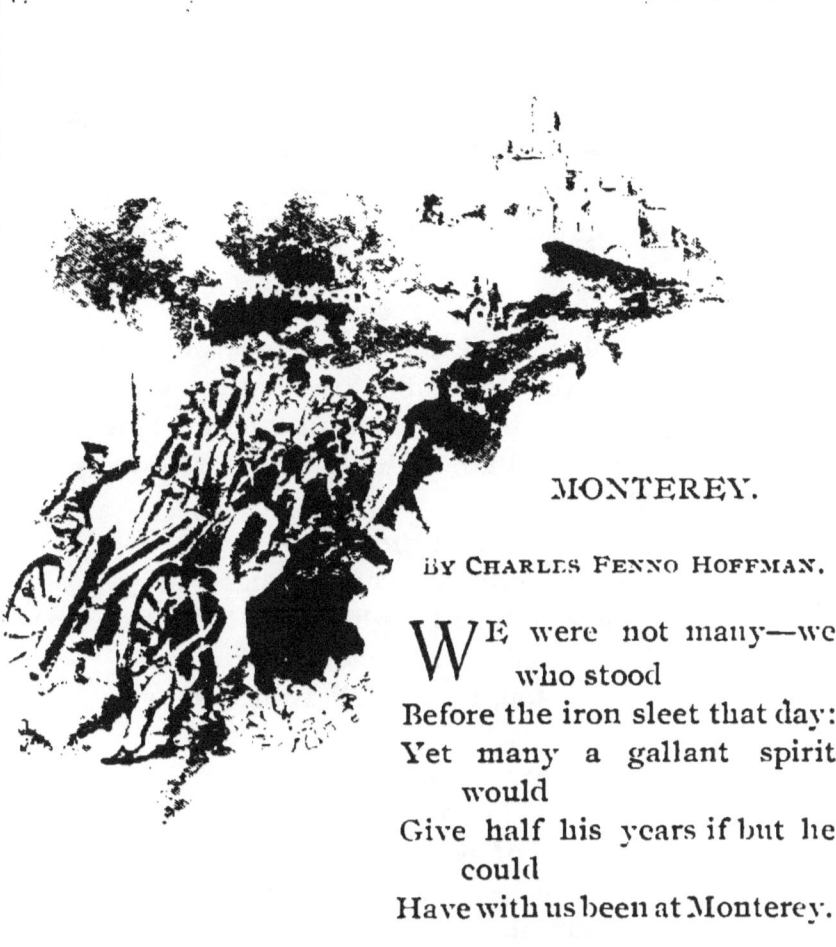

MONTEREY.

BY CHARLES FENNO HOFFMAN.

WE were not many—we
    who stood
Before the iron sleet that day:
Yet many a gallant spirit
    would
Give half his years if but he
    could
Have with us been at Monterey.

Now here, now there, the shot it hail'd
    In deadly drifts of fiery spray,
Yet not a single soldier quail'd
When wounded comrades round them wail'd
    Their dying shout at Monterey.

149

And on—still on our column kept
　　Through walls of flame its withering way ;
Where fell the dead, the living stept,
Still charging on the guns which swept
　　The slippery streets of Monterey.

The foe himself recoil'd aghast,
　　When, striking where he strongest lay,
We swoop'd his flanking batteries past,
And braving full their murderous blast,
　　Storm'd home the towers of Monterey.

Our banners on those turrets wave,
　　And there our evening bugles play :
Where orange-boughs above their grave
Keep green the memory of the brave
　　Who fought and fell at Monterey.

We are not many—we who press'd
　　Beside the brave who fell that day—
But who of us has not confess'd
He 'd rather share their warrior rest
　　Than not have been at Monterey ?

BUENA VISTA.

[By some strange oversight, this fine ballad appears in
none of the popular collections. So far as the editor can
discover, indeed, it exists nowhere in print except in a
volume privately printed by General Pike some years ago,
and to his courtesy the editor is indebted for the copy
from which the piece is here reproduced.—EDITOR.]

BUENA VISTA.

BY ALBERT PIKE.

FROM the Rio Grande's waters to the icy lakes of Maine,
Let all exult! for we have met the enemy again;
Beneath their stern old mountains we have met them in their pride,
And rolled from BUENA VISTA back the battle's bloody tide;
Where the enemy came surging swift, like the Mississippi's flood,
And the reaper, Death, with strong arms swung his sickle red with blood.

Santana boasted loudly that, before two hours were
    past,
His Lancers through Saltillo should pursue us fierce and
    fast :—
On comes his solid infantry, line marching after line ;
Lo ! their great standards in the sun like sheets of silver
    shine :
With thousands upon thousands,—yea, with more than
    three to one,—
Their forests of bright bayonets fierce-flashing in the
    sun.

Lo ! Guanajuato's regiment ; Morelos' boasted corps,
And Guadalajara's chosen troops !—all veterans tried
    before.
Lo! galloping upon the right four thousand lances gleam,
Where, floating in the morning-wind, their blood-red
    pennons stream ;
And here his stern artillery climbs up the broad plateau :
To-day he means to strike at us an overwhelming blow.

Now, Wool, hold strongly to the heights ! for, lo ! the
    mighty tide
Comes, thundering like an avalanche, deep, terrible and
    wide.
Now, Illinois, stand steady ! Now, Kentucky, to their
    aid !
For a portion of our line, alas ! is broken and dismayed :

Great bands of shameless fugitives are fleeing from the
field,
And the day is lost, if Illinois and brave Kentucky yield.

One of O'Brien's guns is gone !—On, on their masses
drift,
Till their cavalry and infantry outflank us on the left ;
Our light troops, driven from the hills, retreat in wild
dismay,
And round us gather, thick and dark, the Mexican array.
SANTANA thinks the day is gained ; for, now approaching
near,
MIÑON's dark cloud of Lancers sternly menaces our rear.

Now, LINCOLN, gallant gentleman, lies dead upon the
field,
Who strove to stay those cravens, when before the storm
they reeled.
Fire, WASHINGTON, fire fast and true ! Fire, SHERMAN,
fast and far !
Lo ! BRAGG comes thundering to the front, to breast the
adverse war !
SANTANA thinks the day is gained ! On, on his masses
crowd,
And the roar of battle swells again more terrible and
loud.

NOT YET! Our brave old General comes to regain the
day ;
KENTUCKY, to the rescue ! MISSISSIPPI, to the fray !

Again our line advances! Gallant DAVIS fronts the foe,
And back before his rifles, in red waves the Lancers flow.
Upon them yet once more, ye brave! The avalanche is
     stayed!
Back roll the Aztec multitudes, all broken and dismayed.

Ride! MAY!—To Buena Vista! for the Lancers gain our
     rear,
And we have few troops there to check their vehement
     career.
Charge, ARKANSAS! KENTUCKY, charge! YELL, PORTER,
     VAUGHAN, are slain,   .
But the shattered troops cling desperately unto that
     crimsoned plain;
Till, with the Lancers intermixed, pursuing and pursued,
Westward, in combat hot and close, drifts off the mul-
     titude.

And May comes charging from the hills with his ranks of
     flaming steel,
While shattered with a sudden fire, the foe already reel:
They flee amain!—Now to the left, to stay the torrent
     there,
Or else the day is surely lost, in horror and despair!
For their hosts pour swiftly onward, like a river in the
     spring,
Our flank is turned, and on our left their cannon
     thundering.

Now, good Artillery! bold Dragoons! Steady, brave
hearts, be calm!
Through rain, cold hail, and thunder, now nerve each
gallant arm!
What though their shot fall round us here, yet thicker
than the hail?
We 'll stand against them, as the rock stands firm against
the gale.
Lo! their battery is silenced! but our iron sleet still
showers:
They falter, halt, retreat!—Hurrah! the glorious day is
ours!

In front, too, has the fight gone well, where upon gallant
LANE,
And on stout Mississippi, the thick Lancers charged in
vain:
Ah! brave Third Indiana! you have nobly wiped away
The reproach that through another corps befell your
State to-day;
For back, all broken and dismayed, before your storm of
fire,
SANTANA'S boasted chivalry, a shattered wreck, retire.

Now charge again, SANTANA! or the day is surely lost—
For back, like broken waves, along our left your hordes
are tossed.
Still faster roar his batteries,—his whole reserve moves
on;

More work remains for us to do, ere the good fight is
    won.
Now for your wives and children men! Stand steady yet
    once more!
Fight for your lives and honors! Fight as you never
    fought before!

Ho! HARDIN breasts it bravely! and heroic BISSELL
    there
Stands firm before the storm of balls that fill the aston-
    ished air:
The Lancers dash upon them too! The foe swarm ten to
    one:
HARDIN is slain; MCKEE and CLAY the last time see the
    sun:
And many another gallant heart, in that last desperate
    fray,
Grew cold, its last thought turning to its loved ones far
    away.

Speed, speed, Artillery! to the front!—for the hurricane
    of fire
Crushes those noble regiments, reluctant to retire!
Speed swiftly! Gallop! Ah! they come! Again BRAGG
    climbs the ridge,
And his grape sweeps down the swarming foe, as a strong
    man moweth sedge:

Thus baffled in their last attack, compelled perforce to
   yield,
Still menacing in firm array, their columns leave the
   field.

The guns still roared at intervals; but silence fell at
   last,
And on the dead and dying came the evening shadows
   fast.
And then above the mountains rose the cold moon's sil-
   ver shield,
And patiently and pitying she looked upon the field.
While careless of his wounded, and neglectful of his
   dead,
Despairingly and sullenly by night SANTANA fled.

And thus on BUENA VISTA'S heights a long day's work
   was done,
And thus our brave old General another battle won.
Still, still our glorious banner waves, unstained by flight
   or shame,
And the Mexicans among their hills still tremble at our
   name.
So, HONOR UNTO THOSE THAT STOOD! DISGRACE TO
   THOSE THAT FLED!
AND EVERLASTING GLORY UNTO BUENA VISTA'S
   DEAD!

   February 28, 1847.

THE BIVOUAC OF THE DEAD.

By THEODORE O'HARA.

[Originally written on the occasion of the erection of a monument to the Kentucky volunteers who fell at Buena Vista.—EDITOR.]

THE muffled drum's sad roll has beat
    The soldier's last tattoo ;
No more on Life's parade shall meet
    That brave and fallen few.
On Fame's eternal camping-ground
    Their silent tents are spread,
And Glory guards, with solemn round,
    The bivouac of the dead.

No rumor of the foe's advance
    Now swells upon the wind ;
No troubled thought at midnight haunts
    Of loved ones left behind ;
No vision of the morrow's strife
    The warrior's dream alarms ;
No braying horn nor screaming fife
    At dawn shall call to arms.

Their shivered swords are red with rust ;
  Their plumèd heads are bowed ;
Their haughty banner, trailed in dust,
  Is now their martial shroud.
And plenteous funeral tears have washed
  The red stains from each brow,
And the proud forms, by battle gashed,
  Are free from anguish now.

The neighing troop, the flashing blade,
  The bugle's stirring blast,
The charge, the dreadful cannonade,
  The din and shout are past ;
Nor war's wild note, nor glory's peal,
  Shall thrill with fierce delight
Those breasts that nevermore may feel
  The rapture of the fight.

Like the fierce northern hurricane
  That sweeps his great plateau,
Flushed with the triumph yet to gain,
  Came down the serried foe.
Who heard the thunder of the fray
  Break o'er the field beneath,
Knew well the watchword of that day
  Was " Victory or Death."

Long had the doubtful conflict raged
  O'er all that stricken plain,
For never fiercer fight had waged
  The vengeful blood of Spain ;
And still the storm of battle blew,
  Still swelled the gory tide ;
Not long our stout old chieftain knew,
  Such odds his strength could bide.

'T was in that hour his stern command
  Called to a martyr's grave
The flower of his belovèd land,
  The nation's flag to save.
By rivers of their fathers' gore
  His first-born laurels grew
And well he deemed the sons would pour
  There lives for glory too.

Full many a norther's breath has swept,
  O'er Angostura's plain—
And long the pitying sky has wept
  Above its mouldered slain.
The raven's scream or eagle's flight
  Or shepherd's pensive lay,
Alone awakes each sullen height
  That frowned o'er that dread fray.

Sons of the Dark and Bloody ground,
  Ye must not slumber there,
Where stranger steps and tongues resound
  Along the heedless air.
Your own proud land's heroic soil
  Shall be your fitter grave ;
She claims from war his richest spoil—
  The ashes of her brave.

Thus 'neath their parent turf they rest,
  Far from the gory field,
Borne to a Spartan mother's breast
  On many a bloody shield ;
The sunshine of their native sky
  Smiles sadly on them here,
And kindred eyes and hearts watch by
  The heroes' sepulchre.

Rest on, embalmed and sainted dead !
  Dear as the blood ye gave,
No impious footstep here shall tread
  The herbage of your grave ;
Nor shall your story be forgot,
  While Fame her record keeps,
Or Honor points the hallowed spot
  Where Valor proudly sleeps.

Yon marble minstrel's voiceless stone
  In deathless song shall tell
When many a vanished age hath flown,
  The story how ye fell ;
Nor wreck, nor change, nor winter's blight,
  Nor Time's remorseless doom,
Shall dim one ray of glory's light
  That gilds your deathless tomb.

THE CIVIL WAR

BROTHER JONATHAN'S LAMENT FOR SISTER CAROLINE.

By OLIVER WENDELL HOLMES.

(Written in December, 1860, when South Carolina adopted the Ordinance of Secession.)

SHE has gone,—she has left us in passion and pride—
  Our stormy-browed sister, so long at our side !
She has torn her own star from our firmament's glow,
And turned on her brother the face of a foe !

O Caroline, Caroline, child of the sun,
We can never forget that our hearts have been one,—
Our foreheads both sprinkled in Liberty's name,
From the fountain of blood with the finger of flame !

You were always too ready to fire at a touch ;
But we said: "She's a beauty—she does not mean much."
We have scowled when you uttered some turbulent threat;
But Friendship still whispered: " Forgive and forget."

Has our love all died out?   Have its altars grown cold?
Has the curse come at last which the fathers foretold?
Then Nature must teach us the strength of the chain
That her petulant children would sever in vain.

They may fight till the buzzards are gorged with their
        spoil,—
Till the harvest grows black as it rots in the soil,
Till the wolves and the catamounts troop from their
        caves,
And the shark tracks the pirate, the lord of the waves :

In vain is the strife ! When its fury is past,
Their fortunes must flow in one channel at last,
As the torrents that rush from the mountains of snow
Roll mingled in peace in the valleys below.

Our Union is river, lake, ocean, and sky ;
Man breaks not the medal when God cuts the die !
Though darkened with sulphur, though cloven with
        steel,
The blue arch will brighten, the waters will heal !

O Caroline, Caroline, child of the sun,
There are battles with fate that can never be won !
The star-flowering banner must never be furled,
For its blossoms of light are the hope of the world !

Go, then, our rash sister, afar and aloof,—
Run wild in the sunshine away from our roof;
But when your heart aches and your feet have grown
    sore,
Remember the pathway that leads to our door !

THE TWELFTH OF APRIL.

A.D., 1861.

BY EDMUND CLARENCE STEDMAN.

[Peculiar interest attaches to this piece as the first poem written after the actual outbreak of the Civil War and inspired by its events. The poem appeared in the evening edition of the New York *World*, on April 16, 1861.—EDITOR.]

CAME the morning of that day,
    When the God to whom we pray,
Gave the soul of Henry Clay
    To the land ;
How we loved him—living, dying!
But his birthday banners flying,
Saw us asking and replying,
    Hand to hand.

For we knew that far away,
Round the fort at Charleston bay,
Hung the dark impending fray,
    Soon to fall;

And that Sumter's brave defender
Had the summons to surrender :
Seventy loyal hearts and tender—
    That was all.

And we knew the April sun
Lit the length of many a gun—
Hosts of batteries to the one
    Island crag ;

Guns and mortars grimly frowning,
Johnson, Moultrie, Pinckney, crowning,
And ten thousand men disowning
    The old flag.

O the fury of the fight
Even then was at its height !
Yet no breath from noon till night
    Reached us here ;
We had almost ceased to wonder,
And the day had faded under,
When—the echo of the thunder
    Filled each ear !

Then our hearts more fiercely beat,
As we crowded on the street,
Hot to gather and repeat
    All the tale ;
All the doubtful chances turning,
Till our souls with shame were burning,
As if all our bitter yearning
    Could avail !

Who had fired the earliest gun ?
Was the fort by traitors won ?
Was there succor ? What was done,
    Who could know?

And once more our thoughts would wander
To the gallant, lone commander,
On his battered ramparts grander
    Than the foe.

Not too long the brave shall wait :
On their own heads be their fate,
Who against the hallowed State
    Dare begin ;
Flag defied and compact riven !
In the record of high Heaven,
How shall southern men be shriven
    For the sin !

MEN OF THE NORTH AND WEST.

BY RICHARD HENRY STODDARD.

[This poem was the second piece that appeared in print after the fall of Fort Sumter. It was published in the *World* on the day after the appearance of Mr. Stedman's "The Twelfth of April."--EDITOR.]

MEN of the North and West,
 Wake in your might.
Prepare, as the rebels have done,
 For the fight !
You cannot shrink from the test ;
Rise ! Men of the North and West !

They have torn down your banner of stars ;
 They have trampled the laws ;
They have stifled the freedom they hate,
 For no cause !
Do you love it or slavery best ?
Speak ! Men of the North and West !

They strike at the life of the State :
    Shall the murder be done ?
They cry : " We are two ! " And you ?
    " We are one ! "
You must meet them, then, breast to breast ;
On ! Men of the North and West !

Not with words ; they laugh them to scorn,
    And tears they despise ;
But with swords in your hands, and death
    In your eyes !
Strike home ! leave to God all the rest ;
Strike ! Men of the North and West !

RHODE ISLAND TO THE SOUTH.

BY GENERAL F. W. LANDER.

ONCE, on New England's bloody heights,
  And o'er a southern plain,
Our fathers fought for sovereign rights,
  That working men might reign.

And by that only Lord we serve,
  The great Jehovah's name ;
By those sweet lips that ever nerve
  High hearts to deeds of fame ;

By all that makes the man a king,
  The household hearth a throne,—
Take back the idle scoff ye fling,
  Where freedom claims its own.

For though our battle hope was vague
  Upon Manassas' plain,
Where Slocum stood with gallant Sprague
  And gave his life in vain,—

Before we yield the holy trust
　Our old forefathers gave,
Or wrong New England's hallowed dust,
　Or grant the wrongs ye crave,—

We 'll print in kindred gore so deep
　The shore we love to tread,
That woman's eyes shall fail to weep
　O'er man's unnumbered dead.

OUR COUNTRY'S CALL.

By WILLIAM CULLEN BRYANT.

L AY down the axe, fling by the spade ;
    Leave in its track the toiling plough ;
The rifle and the bayonet-blade
   For arms like yours were fitter now ;
And let the hands that ply the pen
   Quit the light task, and learn to wield
The horseman's crooked brand, and rein
   The charger on the battle-field.

Our country calls ; away ! away !
   To where the blood-stream blots the green ;
Strike to defend the gentlest sway
   That Time in all his course has seen.
See, from a thousand coverts—see
   Spring the armed foes that haunt her track ;
They rush to smite her down, and we
   Must beat the banded traitors back.

Ho ! sturdy as the oaks ye cleave,
   And moved as soon to fear and flight,

Men of the glade and forest ! leave
  Your woodcraft for the field of fight.
The arms that wield the axe must pour
  An iron tempest on the foe ;
His serried ranks shall reel before
  The arm that lays the panther low.

And ye who breast the mountain storm
  By grassy steep or highland lake,
Come, for the land ye love, to form
  A bulwark that no foe can break.
Stand, like your own gray cliffs that mock
  The whirlwind ; stand in her defence :
The blast as soon shall move the rock,
  As rushing squadrons bear ye thence.

And ye whose homes are by her grand
  Swift rivers, rising far away,
Come from the depth of her green land
  As mighty in your march as they ;
As terrible as when the rains
  Have swelled them over bank and bourne,
With sudden floods to drown the plains
  And sweep along the woods uptorn.

And ye who throng beside the deep,
  Her ports and hamlets of the strand,
In number like the waves that leap
  On his long-murmuring marge of sand,

Come, like that deep, when, o'er his brim,
   He rises, all his floods to pour,
And flings the proudest barks that swim,
   A helpless wreck against his shore.

Few, few were they whose swords of old
   Won the fair land in which we dwell;
But we are many, we who hold
   The grim resolve to guard it well.
Strike for that broad and goodly land,
   Blow after blow, till men shall see
That Might and Right move hand in hand,
   And Glorious must their triumph be.

A CRY TO ARMS.

By HENRY TIMROD.

HO, woodsmen of the mountain-side!
  Ho, dwellers in the vales!
Ho, ye who by the chafing tide
  Have roughened in the gales!
Leave barn and byre, leave kin and cot,
  Lay by the bloodless spade;
Let desk and case and counter rot,
  And burn your books of trade!

The despot roves your fairest lands;
  And till he flies or fears,
Your fields must grow but armèd bands,
  Your sheaves be sheaves of spears!
Give up to mildew and to rust
  The useless tools of gain,
And feed your country's sacred dust
  With floods of crimson rain!

Come with the weapons at your call—
  With musket, pike, or knife ;
He wields the deadliest blade of all
  Who lightest holds his life.
The arm that drives its unbought blows
  With all a patriot's scorn,
Might brain a tyrant with a rose
  Or stab him with a thorn.

Does any falter ? Let him turn
  To some brave maiden's eyes,
And catch the holy fires that burn
  In those sublunar skies.
Oh, could you like your women feel,
  And in their spirit march,
A day might see your lines of steel
  Beneath the victor's arch !

What hope, O God ! would not grow warm
  When thoughts like these give cheer?
The lily calmly braves the storm,
  And shall the palm-tree fear ?
No ! rather let its branches court
  The rack that sweeps the plain ;
And from the lily's regal port
' Learn how to breast the strain.

Ho, woodsmen of the mountain-side!
　Ho, dwellers in the vales!
Ho, ye who by the roaring tide
　Have roughened in the gales!
Come, flocking gayly to the fight,
　From forest, hill, and lake;
We battle for our country's right,
　And for the lily's sake!

[Southern.]

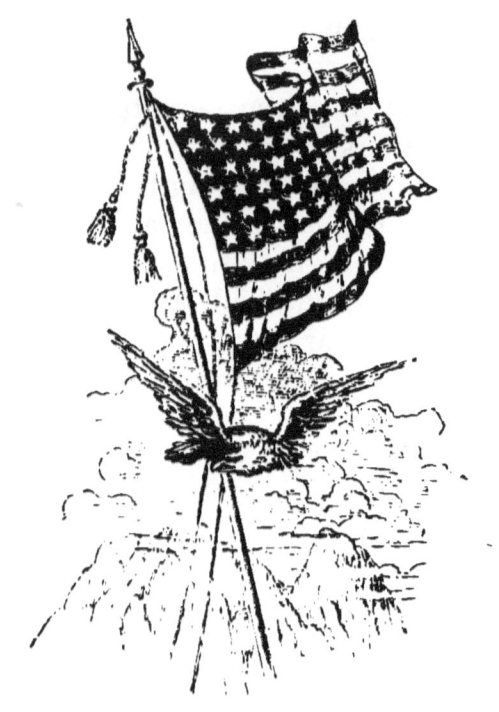

THE BANNER OF THE STARS.

By R. W. RAYMOND.

HURRAH! boys, hurrah! fling our banner to the breeze!
Let the enemies of freedom see its folds again unfurled.
And down with the pirates that scorn upon the seas
Our victorious Yankee banner, sign of Freedom to the World!

Chorus.—We 'll never have a new flag, for ours is the
true flag,
The true flag, the true flag, the Red, White, and Blue
flag,
Hurrah! boys, hurrah! we will carry to the wars,
The old flag, the free flag, the Banner of the Stars.

And what tho' its white shall be crimsoned with our
blood?
And what tho' its stripes shall be shredded in the
storms?
To the torn flag, the worn flag, we 'll keep our promise
good,
And we 'll bear the starry blue field, with gallant hearts
and arms.

—Chorus.

Then, cursed be he who would strike our Starry Flag!
May the God of Hosts be with us, as we smite the
traitor down!
And cursed be he who would hesitate or lag,
Till the dear flag, the fair flag, with Victory we crown.

Chorus.

THE FLAG OF THE CONSTELLATION.

By T. BUCHANAN REID.

THE stars of our morn on our banner borne,
　　With the iris of heav'n are blended,
The hands of our sires first mingled those fires,
　　By us they shall be defended !
Then hail the true—the Red, White, and Blue,
　　The flag of the Constellation ;
It sails as it sailed, by our fore-fathers hailed,
　　O'er battles that made us a nation.

What hand so bold to strike from its fold,
　　One star or stripe of its bright'ning ;
To him be each star a fiery Mars,
　　Each stripe a terrible lightning.
Then hail the true—the Red, White, and Blue,
　　The flag of the Constellation.
It sails as it sailed, by our fore-fathers hailed,
　　O'er battles that made us a nation.

Its meteor form shall ride the storm
   Till the fiercest of foes surrender;
The storm gone by, it shall gild the sky,
   As a rainbow of peace and splendor.
Then hail the true—the Red, White, and Blue,
   The flag of the Constellation,
It sails as it sailed, by our fore-fathers hailed,
   O'er battles that made us a nation.

Peace, peace to the world—is our motto unfurled,
   Tho' we shun not a field that is gory;
At home or abroad, fearing none but our God,
   We will carve our own pathway to glory!
Then hail the true—the Red, White, and Blue,
   The flag of the Constellation,
It sails as it sailed, by our fore-fathers hailed,
   O'er battles that made us a nation.

Florence, Italy, May, 1861.

THE STARS AND STRIPES.

BY JAMES T. FIELDS.

RALLY round the flag, boys—
 Give it to the breeze !
That 's the banner we bore
 On the land and seas.

Brave hearts are under it,
 Let the *traitors* brag,
Gallant lads, fire away !
 And fight for the flag.

Their flag is but a rag—
 Ours is the true one ;
Up with the Stars and Stripes !
 Down with the new one !

Let our colors fly, boys—
 Guard them day and night ;
For victory is liberty,
 And God will bless the right.

THE BONNIE BLUE FLAG.

BY ANNIE CHAMBERS KETCHUM.

COME, brothers! rally for the right!
 The bravest of the brave
Sends forth her ringing battle-cry
 Beside the Atlantic wave!
She leads the way in honor's path;
 Come brothers, near and far,
Come rally round the Bonnie Blue Flag
 That bears a single star!

We 've borne the Yankee trickery,
 The Yankee gibe and sneer,
Till Yankee insolence and pride
 Know neither shame nor fear;
But ready now with shot and steel
 Their brazen front to mar,
We hoist aloft the Bonnie Blue Flag
 That bears a single star.

Now Georgia marches to the front,
  And close beside her come
Her sisters by the Mexique Sea,
  With pealing trump and drum ;
Till answering back from hill and glen
  The rallying cry afar,
A Nation hoists the Bonnie Blue Flag
  That bears a single star !

By every stone in Charleston Bay,
  By each beleaguered town,
We swear to rest not, night nor day,
  But hunt the tyrants down !
Till bathed in valor's holy blood
  The gazing world afar
Shall greet with shouts the Bonnie Blue Flag
  That bears the cross and star !

[Southern.]

THE STRIPES AND THE STARS.

BY EDNA DEAN PROCTOR.

O STAR-SPANGLED BANNER! the flag of our
pride!
Though trampled by traitors and basely defied,
Fling out to the glad winds your red, white, and blue,
For the heart of the Northland is beating for you!
And her strong arm is nerving to strike with a will,
Till the foe and his boastings are humbled and still!
Here's welcome to wounding and combat and scars
And the glory of death—for the Stripes and the Stars!

From prairie, O ploughman! speed boldly away—
There's seed to be sown in God's furrows to-day!
Row landward, lone fisher! stout woodman come home!
Let smith leave his anvil and weaver his loom,
And hamlet and city ring loud with the cry:
"For God and our country we'll fight till we die!
Here's welcome to wounding and combat and scars
And the glory of death—for the Stripes and the Stars!"

Invincible banner! the flag of the free,
Oh, where treads the foot that would falter for thee?
Or the hands to be folded, till triumph is won
And the eagle looks proud, as of old, to the sun?
Give tears for the parting—a murmur of prayer—
Then forward! the fame of our standard to share!
With welcome to wounding and combat and scars
And the glory of death—for the Stripes and the Stars!

O God of our fathers! this banner must shine
Where battle is hottest, in warfare divine!
The cannon has thundered, the bugle has blown—
We fear not the summons—we fight not alone!
O lead us, till wide from the gulf to the sea
The land shall be sacred to freedom and Thee!
With love for oppression; with blessing, for scars—
One country—one banner—the Stripes and the Stars!

DIXIE.

By ALBERT PIKE.

SOUTHRONS, hear your country call you !
  Up, lest worse than death befall you !
To arms ! To arms ! To arms, in Dixie !
Lo ! all the beacon-fires are lighted—
Let all hearts be now united !
To arms ! To arms ! To arms, in Dixie !
    Advance the flag of Dixie !
    Hurrah ! hurrah !
    For Dixie's land we take our stand,
    And live or die for Dixie !
    To arms ! To arms !
    And conquer peace for Dixie !
    To arms ! To arms !
    And conquer peace for Dixie !

Hear the Northern thunders mutter !
Northern flags in South winds flutter !
    To arms !

Send them back your fierce defiance!
Stamp upon the accursed alliance!
    To arms!
    Advance the flag of Dixie!

Fear no danger! shun no labor!
Lift up rifle, pike, and sabre!
    To arms!
Shoulder pressing close to shoulder,
Let the odds make each heart bolder!
    To arms!
    Advance the flag of Dixie!

How the South's great heart rejoices
At your cannon's ringing voices!
    To arms!
For faith betrayed, and pledges broken,
Wrongs inflicted, insults spoken,
    To arms!
    Advance the flag of Dixie!

Strong as lions, swift as eagles,
Back to their kennels hunt these beagles!
    To arms!
Cut the unequal bond asunder!
Let them hence each other plunder!
    To arms!
    Advance the flag of Dixie!

Swear upon your country's altar
Never to submit or falter!
  To arms!
Till the spoilers are defeated,
Till the Lord's work is completed,
  To arms!
  Advance the flag of Dixie!

Halt not till our Federation
Secures among earth's powers its station!
  To arms!
Then at peace, and crowned with glory,
Hear your children tell the story!
  To arms!
  Advance the flag of Dixie!

If the loved ones weep in sadness,
Victory soon shall bring them gladness.
  To arms!
Exultant pride soon vanish sorrow;
Smiles chase tears away to-morrow.
To arms! To arms! To arms, in Dixie!
  Advance the flag of Dixie!
  Hurrah! hurrah!
  For Dixie's land we take our stand,
  And live or die for Dixie!

To arms! To arms
And conquer peace for Dixie!
To arms! To arms!
And conquer peace for Dixie!

[Southern.]

THE OATH OF FREEDOM.

By JAMES BARRON HOPE.

BORN free, thus we resolve to live :
 By Heaven, we will be free !
By all the stars which burn on high—
By the green earth—the mighty sea—
By God's unshaken majesty,
　　We will be free or die !
　　Then let the drums all roll !
　　Let all the trumpets blow !
　　Mind, heart, and soul,
　　We spurn control
　　Attempted by a foe !

Born free, thus we resolve to live :
By Heaven, we will be free !
And, vainly now the Northmen try
To beat us down—in arms we stand
To strike for this our native land !
　　We will be free or die !
　　Then let the drums all roll !

197

Born free, we thus resolve to live :
By Heaven, we will be free !
Our wives and children look on high,
Pray God to smile upon the right !
And bid us in the deadly fight
        As freemen live or die !
        Then let the drums all roll !

Born free, thus we resolve to live :
By Heaven, we will be free !
And ere we cease this battle-cry,
Be all our blood, our kindred's spilt,
On bayonet or sabre hilt !
        We will be free or die !
        Then let the drums all roll !

Born free, thus we resolve to live :
By Heaven, we will be free !
Defiant let the banners fly,
Shake out their glories to the air,
And kneeling, brothers, let us swear
        We will be free or die !
        Then let the drums all roll !

Born free, thus we resolve to live :
By Heaven, we will be free !

And to this oath the dead reply—
Our valiant fathers' sacred ghosts—
These with us, and the God of hosts,
We will be free or die !
Then let the drums all roll !

[Southern.]

By CHARLES DAWSON SHANLY.

[In many collections this poem is entitled "The Fancy
Shot." It was first published in London, in the paper
called *Once-a-Week*, and was there entitled "Civile Bel-
lum." It is believed to be the work of Charles Dawson
Shanly, who died in 1876.—EDITOR.]

" RIFLEMAN, shoot me a fancy shot
    Straight at the heart of yon prowling vidette;
Ring me a ball in the glittering spot
    That shines on his breast like an amulet ! ' "

" Ah, captain ! here goes for a fine-drawn bead,
　　There 's music around when my barrel 's in tune ! "
Crack ! went the rifle, the messenger sped,
　　And dead from his horse fell the ringing dragoon.

" Now, rifleman, steal through the bushes, and snatch
　　From your victim some trinket to handsel first blood ;
A button, a loop, or that luminous patch
　　That gleams in the moon like a diamond stud ! "

" O captain ! I staggered and sunk on my track,
　　When I gazed on the face of that fallen vidette,
For he looked so like you, as he lay on his back,
　　That my heart rose upon me, and masters me yet.

" But I snatched off the trinket,—this locket of gold ;
　　An inch from the centre my lead broke its way,
Scarce grazing the picture, so fair to behold,
　　Of a beautiful lady in bridal array."

" Ha ! rifleman, fling me the locket !—'t is she,
　　My brother's young bride,—and the fallen dragoon
Was her husband—Hush ! soldier, 't was Heaven's decree,
　　We must bury him there, by the light of the moon !

" But hark ! the far bugles their warnings unite ;
　　War is a virtue, weakness a sin ;
There 's a lurking and loping around us to-night ;—
　　Load again, rifleman, keep your hand in ! "

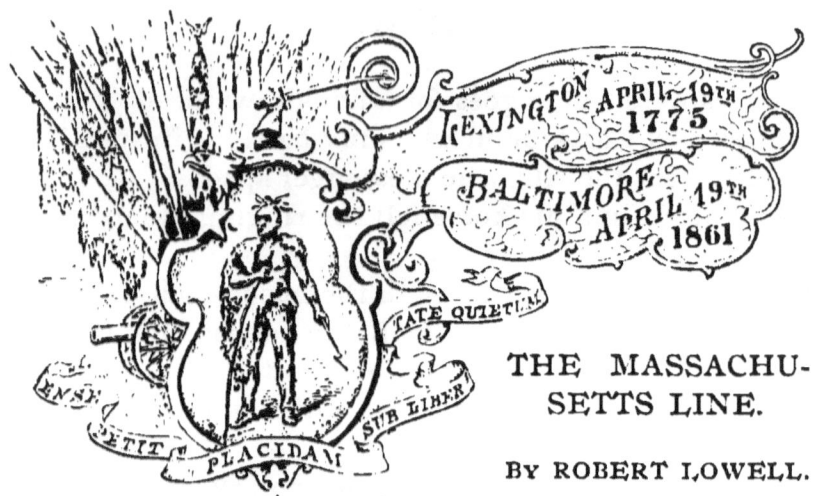

THE MASSACHU-SETTS LINE.

BY ROBERT LOWELL.

STILL first, as long and long ago,
　　Let Massachusetts muster;
Give her the post right next the foe;
　　Be sure that you may trust her.
She was the first to give her blood
　　For freedom and for honor;
She trod her soil to crimson mud;
　　God's blessing be upon her!

She never faltered for the right,
　　Nor ever will hereafter;
Fling up her name with all your might,
　　Shake roof-tree and shake rafter!
But of old deeds she need not brag,
　　How she broke sword and fetter;
Fling out again the old striped flag!
　　She 'll do yet more and better.

In peace her sails fleck all the seas,
  Her mills shake every river ;
And where are scenes so fair as these
  God and her true hands give her ?
Her claim in war who seek to rob ?
  All others come in later ;—
Hers first it is to front the mob,
  The tyrant, and the traitor.

God bless, God bless this glorious State !
  Let her have her way in battle !
She 'll go where batteries crash with fate
  Or where thick rifles rattle.
Give her the Light and let her try,
  And then who can may press her ;
She 'll go straight on or she will die ;
  God bless her, and God bless her !

May 7, 1861.

BETHEL.

BY A. J. H. DUGANNE.

[Theodore Winthrop, a brilliant young man of letters, was killed at Big Bethel, on June 10, 1861.—EDITOR.]

WE mustered at midnight, in darkness we formed,
    And the whisper went round of a fort to be stormed;
But no drum-beat had called us, no trumpet we heard,
And no voice of command, but our colonel's low word—
        "Column! Forward!"

And out, through the mist, and the murk of the morn,
From the beaches of Hampton our barges were borne;
And we heard not a sound, save the sweep of the oar,
Till the word of our colonel came up from the shore—
          "Column ! Forward !"

With hearts bounding bravely, and eyes all alight,
As ye dance to soft music, so trod we that night ;
Through the aisles of the greenwood, with vines over-
     arched,
Tossing dew-drops, like gems, from our feet, as we
     marched—
          "Column ! Forward !"

As ye dance with the damsels, to viol and flute,
So we skipped from the shadows, and mocked their pur-
     suit ;
But the soft zephyrs chased us, with scents of the morn,
As we passed by the hay-fields and green waving corn—
          "Column ! Forward !"

For the leaves were all laden with fragrance of June,
And the flowers and the foliage with sweets were in
     tune ;
And the air was so calm, and the forest so dumb,
That we heard our own heart-beats, like taps of a drum—
          "Column ! Forward !"

Till the lull of the lowlands was stirred by the breeze,
And the buskins of morn brushed the tops of the trees,
And the glintings of glory that slid from her track
By the sheen of our rifles were gayly flung back—
　　　　"Column! Forward!"

And the woodlands grew purple with sunshiny mist,
And the blue-crested hill-tops with rose-light were kissed,
And the earth gave her prayers to the sun in perfumes,
Till we marched as through gardens, and trampled on
　　blooms—
　　　　"Column! Forward!"

Ay, trampled on blossoms, and seared the sweet breath
Of the greenwood with low-brooding vapors of death;
O'er the flowers and the corn we were borne like a blast,
And away to the forefront of battle we passed—
　　　　"Column! Forward!"

For the cannon's hoarse thunder roared out from the
　　glades,
And the sun was like lightning on banners and blades,
When the long line of chanting Zouaves, like a flood,
From the green of the woodlands rolled, crimson as
　　blood—
　　　　"Column! Forward!"

While the sound of their song, like the surge of the seas,
With the " Star-Spangled Banner " swelled over the leas ;
And the sword of Duryea, like a torch, led the way,
Bearing down on the batteries of Bethel that day—
"Column ! Forward ! "

Through green-tasselled cornfields our columns were
thrown,
And like corn by the red scythe of fire we were mown ;
While the cannon's fierce ploughings new-furrowed the
plain,
That our blood might be planted for Liberty's grain—
"Column ! Forward ! "

Oh ! the fields of fair June have no lack of sweet flowers,
But their rarest and best breathe no fragrance like ours ;
And the sunshine of June, sprinkling gold on the corn,
Hath no harvest that ripeneth like Bethel's red morn—
"Column ! Forward ! "

When our heroes, like bridegrooms, with lips and with
breath,
Drank the first kiss of Danger and clasped her in death ;
And the heart of brave Winthrop grew mute with his
lyre,
When the plumes of his genius lay moulting in fire—
"Column ! Forward ! "

Where he fell shall be sunshine as bright as his name,
And the grass where he slept shall be green as his fame;
For the gold of the pen and the steel of the sword
Write his deeds—in his blood—on the land he adored—
          "Column! Forward!"

And the soul of our comrade shall sweeten the air,
And the flowers and the grass-blades his memory upbear;
While the breath of his genius, like music in leaves,
With the corn-tassels whispers, and sings in the sheaves—
          "Column! Forward!"

THE CHARGE BY THE FORD.

By Dr. THOMAS DUNN ENGLISH.

EIGHTY and nine with their captain
  Rode on the enemy's track,
Rode in the gray of the morning:
  Nine of the ninety came back.

Slow rose the mist from the river,
  Lighter each moment the way:
Careless and tearless and fearless
  Galloped they on to the fray.

Singing in tune, how the scabbards
  Loud on the stirrup-irons rang,
Clinked as the men rose in saddle,
  Fell as they sank with a clang,

What is it moves by the river,
  Jaded and weary and weak,
Gray-backs—a cross on their banner—
  Yonder the foe whom they seek.

Silence! They see not, they hear not,
  Tarrying there by the marge:
Forward! Draw sabre! Trot! Gallop!
  Charge! like a hurricane, *charge!*

Ah! 't was a man-trap infernal—
  Fire like the deep pit of hell!
Volley on volley to meet them,
  Mixed with the gray rebels' yell.

Ninety had ridden to battle,
  Tracing the enemy's track,—
Ninety had ridden to battle,
  Nine of the ninety came back.

Honor the name of the ninety;
  Honor the heroes who came
Scathless from five hundred muskets,
  Safe from the lead-bearing flame.

Eighty and one of the troopers
  Lie on the field of the slain—
Lie on the red field of honor:
  Honor the nine who remain!

Cold are the dead there, and gory,
  There where their life-blood was spilt;
Back come the living, each sabre
  Red from the point to the hilt.

Give them three cheers and a tiger!
Let the flags wave as they come!
Give them the blare of the trumpet!
Give them the roll of the drum!

MANASSAS.

July 21, 1861.

BY CATHERINE M. WARFIELD.

THEY have met at last—as storm-clouds
  Meet in heaven,
And the Northmen back and bleeding
  Have been driven :
And their thunders have been stilled,
And their leaders crushed or killed,
And their ranks with terror thrilled,
  Rent and riven !

Like the leaves of Vallambrosa
  They are lying ;
In the moonlight, in the midnight,
  Dead and dying :
Like those leaves before the gale,
Swept their legions, wild and pale ;
While the host that made them quail
  Stood, defying.

When aloft in morning sunlight
      Flags were flaunted,
And "swift vengeance on the rebel"
      Proudly vaunted :
Little did they think that night
Should close upon their shameful flight,
And rebels, victors in the fight,
      Stand undaunted.

But peace to those who perished
      In our passes !
Light be the earth above them ;
      Green the grasses !
Long shall Northmen rue the day
When they met our stern array,
And shrunk from battle's wild affray
      At Manassas.

(Southern.)

UPON THE HILL BEFORE CENTREVILLE.

July 21, 1861.

By GEORGE H. BOKER.

I 'LL tell you what I heard that day :
   I heard the great guns, far away,
Boom after boom. Their sullen sound
Shook all the shuddering air around ;
And shook, ah me ! my shrinking ear,
And downward shook the hanging tear
That, in despite of manhood's pride,
Rolled o'er my face a scalding tide.
And then I prayed. O God ! I prayed,
As never stricken saint, who laid
His hot cheek to the holy tomb
Of Jesus, in the midnight gloom.

"What saw I ?" Little. Clouds of dust ;
Great squares of men, with standards thrust
Against their course ; dense columns crowned
With billowing steel. Then bound on bound,

The long black lines of cannon poured
Behind the horses, streaked and gored
With sweaty speed.   Anon shot by,
Like a lone meteor of the sky,
A single horseman ; and he shone
His bright face on me, and was gone.
All these with rolling drums, with cheers,
With songs familiar to my ears,
Passed under the far-hanging cloud,
And vanished, and my heart was proud !

For mile on mile the line of war
Extended ; and a steady roar,
As of some distant stormy sea,
On the south-wind came up to me.
And high in air, and over all,
Grew, like a fog, that murky pall,
Beneath whose gloom of dusty smoke
The cannon flamed, the bombshell broke.
And the sharp rattling volley rang,
And shrapnel roared, and bullets sang,
And fierce-eyed men, with panting breath,
Toiled onward at the work of death.
I could not see, but knew too well,
That underneath that cloud of hell,
Which still grew more by great degrees,
Man strove with man in deeds like these.

But when the sun had passed his stand
At noon, behold ! on every hand
The dark brown vapor backward bore,
And fainter came the dreadful roar
From the huge sea of striving men.
Thus spoke my rising spirit then :
" Take comfort from that dying sound,
Faint heart, the foe is giving ground ! "
And one, who taxed his horse's powers,
Flung at me, " Ho ! the day is ours ! "
And scoured along.   So swift his pace,
I took no memory of his face.
Then turned I once again to Heaven ;
All things appeared so just and even ;
So clearly from the highest Cause
Traced I the downward-working laws—
Those moral springs, made evident,
In the grand, triumph-crowned event.
So half I shouted, and half sang,
Like Jephtha's daughter, to the clang
Of my spread, cymbal-striking palms,
Some fragments of thanksgiving psalms.

Meanwhile a solemn stillness fell
Upon the land.   O'er hill and dell
Failed every sound.   My heart stood still,
Waiting before some coming ill.
The silence was more sad and dread,
Under that canopy of lead,

Than the wild tumult of the war
That raged a little while before.
All nature, in her work of death,
Paused for one last, despairing breath ;
And, cowering to the earth, I drew
From her strong breast my strength anew.

When I arose, I wondering saw
Another dusty vapor draw,
From the far right, its sluggish way
Toward the main cloud, that frowning lay
Against the western sloping sun :
And all the war was re-begun,
Ere this fresh marvel of my sense
Caught from my mind significance.
And then—why ask me ?   O my God !
Would I had lain beneath the sod,
A patient clod, for many a day,
And from my bones and mouldering clay
The rank field grass and flowers had sprung,
Ere the base sight, that struck and stung
My very soul, confronted me,
Shamed at my own humanity.
O happy dead ! who early fell,
Ye have no wretched tale to tell
Of causeless fear and coward flight,
Of victory snatched beneath your sight,
Of martial strength and honor lost,
Of mere life bought at any cost,

Of the deep, lingering mark of shame,
For ever scorched on brow and name,
That no new deeds, however bright,
Shall banish from men's loathful sight!

Ye perished in your conscious pride,
Ere this vile scandal opened wide
A wound that cannot close nor heal.
Ye perished steel to levelled steel,
Stern votaries of the god of war,
Filled with his godhead to the core!
Ye died to live, these lived to die,
Beneath the scorn of every eye!
How eloquent your voices sound
From the low chambers under ground!
How clear each separate title burns
From your high-set and laurelled urns!
While these, who walk about the earth,
Are blushing at their very birth!
And, though they talk, and go, and come,
Their moving lips are worse than dumb.
Ye sleep beneath the valley's dew,
And all the nation mourns for you;
So sleep till God shall wake the lands!
For angels, armed with fiery brands,
Await to take you by the hands.

The right-hand vapor broader grew;
It rose, and joined itself unto

The main cloud with a sudden dash.
Loud and more near the cannon's crash
Came toward me, and I heard a sound
As if all hell had broken bound—
A cry of agony and fear.
Still the dark vapor rolled more near,
Till at my very feet it tossed,
The vanward fragments of our host.
Can man, Thy image, sink so low,
Thou, who hast bent Thy tinted bow
Across the storm and raging main ;
Whose laws both loosen and restrain
The powers of earth, without whose will
No sparrow's little life is still?
Was fear of hell, or want of faith,
Or the brute's common dread of death
The passion that began a chase,
Whose goal was ruin and disgrace?
What tongue the fearful sight may tell?
What horrid nightmare ever fell
Upon the restless sleep of crime—
What history of another time—
What dismal vision, darkly seen
By the stern-featured Florentine,
Can give a hint to dimly draw
The likeness of the scene I saw?
I saw, yet saw not.   In that sea,
That chaos of humanity,
No more the eye could catch and keep

A single point, than on the deep
The eye may mark a single wave,
Where hurrying myriads leap and rave.
Men of all arms, and all costumes,
Bare-headed, decked with broken plumes ;
Soldiers and officers, and those
Who wore but civil-suited clothes ;
On foot or mounted—some bestrode
Steeds severed from their harnessed load ;
Wild mobs of white-topped wagons, cars,
Of wounded, red with bleeding scars ;
The whole grim panoply of war
Surged on me with a deafening roar !
All shades of fear, disfiguring man,
Glared through their faces' brazen tan.
Not one a moment paused, or stood
To see what enemy pursued.
With shrieks of fear, and yells of pain,
With every muscle on the strain,
Onward the struggling masses bore.
Oh ! had the foemen lain before,
They 'd trampled them to dust and gore,
And swept their lines and batteries
As autumn sweeps the windy trees !
Here one cast forth his wounded friend,
And with his sword or musket-end
Urged on the horses ; there one trod
Upon the likeness of his God,
As if 't were dust ; a coward here

Grew valiant with his very fear,
And struck his weaker comrade prone,
And struggled to the front alone.
All had one purpose, one sole aim,
That mocked the decency of shame,—
To fly, by any means to fly;
They cared not how, they asked not why.
I found a voice.   My burning blood
Flamed up.   Upon a mound I stood ;
I could no more restrain my voice
Than could the prophet of God's choice.
"Back, animated dirt !" I cried,
"Back, on your wretched lives, and hide
Your shame beneath your native clay !
Or if the foe affrights you, slay
Your own base selves ; and, dying, leave
Your children's tearful cheeks to grieve,
Not quail and blush, when you shall come,
Alive, to their degraded home !
Your wives will look askance with scorn ;
Your boys, and infants yet unborn,
Will curse you to God's holy face !
Heaven holds no pardon in its grace
For cowards.   Oh ! are such as ye
The guardians of our liberty ?
Back, if one trace of manhood still
May nerve your arm and brace your will !
You stain your country in the eyes
Of Europe and her monarchies !

The despots laugh, the peoples groan ;
Man's cause is lost and overthrown !
I curse you, by the sacred blood
That freely poured its purple flood
Down Bunker's heights, on Monmouth's plain,
From Georgia to the rocks of Maine !
I curse you, by the patriot band
Whose bones are crumbling in the land !
By those who saved what these had won—
In the high name of Washington ! ' '
Then I remember little more.
As the tide's rising waves, that pour
Over some low and rounded rock,
The coming mass, with one great shock,
Flowed o'er the shelter of my mound,
And raised me helpless from the ground.
As the huge shouldering billows bear,
Half in the sea and half in air,
A swimmer on their foaming crest,
So the foul throng beneath me pressed,
Swept me along, with curse and blow,
And flung me—where, I ne'er shall know.

When I awoke, a steady rain
Made rivulets across the plain ;
And it was dark—oh, very dark.
I was so stunned as scarce to mark
The ghostly figures of the trees,
Or hear the sobbing of the breeze

That flung the wet leaves to and fro.
Upon me lay a dismal woe,
A boundless, superhuman grief,
That drew no promise of relief
From any hope.   Then I arose,
As one who struggles up from blows
By unseen hands ; and as I stood
Alone, I thought that God was good,
To hide, in clouds and driving rain,
Our low world from the angel train,
Whose souls filled heroes when the earth
Was worthy of their noble birth.
By that dull instinct of the mind,
Which leads aright the helpless blind,
I struggled onward, till the dawn
Across the eastern clouds had drawn
A narrow line of watery gray ;
And full before my vision lay
The great dome's gaunt and naked bones
Beneath whose crown the nation thrones
Her queenly person.   On I stole,
With hanging head and abject soul,
Across the high embattled ridge,
And o'er the arches of the bridge.
So freshly pricked my sharp disgrace,
I feared to meet the human face,
Skulking, as any woman might,
Who 'd lost her virtue in the night,
And sees the dreadful glare of day

Prepare to light her homeward way,
Alone, heart-broken, shamed, undone,
I staggered into Washington !
Since then long sluggish days have passed,
And on the wings of every blast
Have come the distant nations' sneers
To tingle in our blushing ears.
In woe and ashes, as was meet,
We wore the penitential sheet.
But now I breathe a purer air,
And from the depths of my despair
Awaken to a cheering morn,
Just breaking through the night forlorn,
A morn of hopeful victory.
Awake, my countrymen, with me !
Redeem the honor which you lost.
With any blood, at any cost !
I ask not how the war began,
Nor how the quarrel branched and ran
To this dread height.   The wrong or right
Stands clear before God's faultless sight.
I only feel the shameful blow,
I only see the scornful foe,
And vengeance burns in every vein
To die, or wipe away the stain.
The war-wise hero of the west,
Wearing his glories as a crest,
Of trophies gathered in your sight,
Is arming for the coming fight.

Full well his wisdom apprehends
The duty and its mighty ends ;
The great occasion of the hour,
That never lay in human power
Since over Yorktown's tented plain
The red cross fell, nor rose again.
My humble pledge of faith I lay,
Dear comrade of my school-boy day,
Before thee, in the nation's view,
And if thy prophet prove untrue,
And from our country's grasp be thrown
The sceptre and the starry crown,
And thou, and all thy marshalled host
Be baffled and in ruin lost ;
Oh ! let me not outlive the blow
That seals my country's overthrow !
And, lest this woful end come true,
Men of the North, I turn to you.
Display your vaunted flag once more,
Southward your eager columns pour !
Sound trump, and fife, and rallying drum ;
From every hill and valley come.
Old men, yield up your treasured gold !
Can liberty be priced and sold ?
Fair matrons, maids, and tender brides
Gird weapons to your lovers' sides ;
And though your hearts break at the deed,
Give them your blessing and God-speed ;
Then point them to the field of flame,

With words like those of Sparta's dame ;
And when the ranks are full and strong,
And the whole army moves along,
A vast result of care and skill,
Obedient to the master will ;
And your young hero draws the sword,
And gives the last commanding word
That hurls your strength upon the foe—
Oh ! let them need no second blow.
Strike, as your fathers struck of old ;
Through summer's heat, and winter's cold ;
Through pain, disaster, and defeat ;
Through marches tracked with bloody feet ;
Through every ill that could befall
The holy cause that bound them all !
Strike as they struck for liberty !
Strike as they struck to make you free !
Strike for the crown of victory !

END OF VOL. I.

Knickerbocker Nuggets.

NUGGET—"A diminutive mass of precious metal."

" Little gems of bookmaking."—*Commercial Gazette*, Cincinnati.

" For many a long day nothing has been thought out or worked out so sure to prove entirely pleasing to cultured book-lovers."—*The Bookmaker*.

I—Gesta Romanorum. Tales of the old monks. Edited by C. SWAN . . . $1 00

" This little gem is a collection of stories composed by the monks of old, who were in the custom of relating them to each other after meals for their mutual amusement and information."—*Williams' Literary Monthly*.

" Nuggets indeed, and charming ones, are these rescued from the mine of old Latin, which would certainly have been lost to many busy readers who can only take what comes to them without delving for hidden treasures."

II—Headlong Hall and Nightmare Abbey. By THOMAS LOVE PEACOCK . . . $1 00

" It must have been the court librarian of King Oberon who originally ordered the series of quaintly artistic little volumes that Messrs. Putnam are publishing under the name of Knickerbocker Nuggets. There is an elfin dignity in the aspect of these books in their bindings of dark and light blue with golden arabesques."—*Portland Press*.

III—Gulliver's Travels. By JONATHAN SWIFT. A reprint of the early complete edition. Very fully illustrated. Two vols. $2 50

" Messrs. Putnam have done a substantial service to all readers of English classics by reprinting in two dainty and artistically bound volumes those biting satires of Jonathan Swift, ' Gulliver's Travels.' "

IV—**Tales from Irving.** With illustrations. Two vols. Selected from " The Sketch Book," " Traveller," " Wolfert's Roost," " Bracebridge Hall." $2 00

" The tales, pathetic and thrilling as they are in themselves, are rendered winsome and realistic by the lifelike portraitures which profusely illustrate the volumes. . . . We confess our high appreciation of the superb manner in which the publishers have got up and sent forth the present volumes—which are real treasures, to be prized for their unique character."—*Christian Union.*

" Such books as these will find their popularity confined to no one country, but they must be received with enthusiasm wherever art and literature are recognized."—*Albany Argus.*

⌐ V—**Book of British Ballads.** Edited by S. C. HALL. A fac-simile of the original edition. With illustrations by CRESWICK, GILBERT, and others $1 50

" This is a diminutive fac-simile of the original very valuable edition. . . . The collection is not only the most complete and reliable that has been published, but the volume is beautifully illustrated by skilful artists."—*Pittsburg Chronicle.*

" Probably the best general collection of our ballad literature, in moderate compass, that has yet been made."—*Chicago Dial.*

✓VI—**The Travels of Baron Münchausen.** Reprinted from the early, complete edition. Very fully illustrated $1 25

" The venerable Baron Münchausen in his long life has never appeared as well-dressed, so far as we know, as now in this goodly company."

" The Baron's stories are as fascinating as the Arabian Nights."—*Church Union.*

VII—**Letters, Sentences, and Maxims.** By Lord CHESTERFIELD. With a critical essay by C. A. SAINTE-BEUVE $1 00

"Full of wise things, quaint things, witty and shrewd things, and the maker of this book has put the pick of them all together."—*London World.*

"Each of the little volumes in this series is a literary gem." —*Christian at Work.*

VIII—**The Vicar of Wakefield.** By GOLD-SMITH. With 32 illustrations by WILLIAM MUL-READY $1 00

"Goldsmith's charming tale seems more charming than ever in the dainty dress of the 'Knickerbocker Nuggets' series. These little books are a delight to the eye, and their convenient form and size make them most attractive to all book-lovers."—*The Writer*, Boston.

"A gem of an edition, well made, printed in clear, readable type, illustrated with spirit, and just such a booklet as, when one has it in his pocket, makes all the difference between solitude and loneliness."—*Independent.*

IX—**Lays of Ancient Rome.** By THOMAS BABINGTON MACAULAY. Illustrated by GEORGE SCHARF $1 00

"The poems included in this collection are too well known to require that attention should be drawn to them, but the beautiful setting which they receive in the dainty cover and fine workmanship of this series makes it a pleasure even to handle the volume."—*Yale Literary Magazine.*

X—**The Rose and the Ring.** By WILLIAM M. THACKERAY. With the author's illustrations. $1 25

"'The Rose and the Ring,' by Thackeray, is reproduced with quaint illustrations, evidently taken from the author's own handiwork."—*Rochester Post-Express.*

XI—Irish Melodies and Songs. By THOMAS MOORE. Illustrated by MACLISE .   . $1 50

" The latest issue is a collection of Thomas Moore's ' Irish Melodies and Songs,' fully aud excellently illustrated, with each page of the text printed within an outline border of appropriate green tint, embellished with emblems and figures fitting the text."—*Boston Times.*

XII—Undine and Sintram. By DE LA MOTTE FOUQUÉ. Illustrated .   .   . $1 00

"' Undine and Sintram ' are the latest issue, bound in one volume. They are of the size classics should be—pocket volumes,—and nothing more desirable is to be found among the new editions of old treasures."—*San José Mercury.*

XIII—The Essays of Elia. By CHARLES LAMB. Two vols.   .   .   . $2 00

" The genial essayist himself could have dreamed of no more beautiful setting than the Putnams have given the *Essays of Elia* by printing them among their Knickerbocker Nuggets."—*Chicago Advance.*

XIV—Tales from the Italian Poets. By LEIGH HUNT. Two vols.   .   . $2 00

" The perfection of artistic bookmaking."—*San Francisco Chronicle.*

" This work is most delightful literature, which finds a fitting place in this collection, bound in volumes of striking beauty."—*Troy Times.*

" Hunt had just that delightful knowledge of the Italian poets that one would most desire for oneself, together with an exquisite style of his own wherein to make his presentation of them to English readers perfect."—*New York Critic.*

The first series, comprising the foregoing eighteen volumes, in handsome case, $19.00

XV.—**Thoughts of the Emperor Marcus Aurelius Antoninus.** Translated by GEORGE LONG $1 00

" The thoughts of the famous Roman are worthy of a new introduction to the army of readers through a volume so dainty and pleasing."—*Intelligencer.*

" As a book for hard study, as a book to inspire reverie, as a book for five minutes or an hour, it is both delightful and profitable."—*Journal of Education.*

" It is an interesting little book, and we feel indebted to the translator for this presentation of his work."—*Presbyterian.*

XVI.—**Æsop's Fables.** Rendered chiefly from original sources. By Rev. THOMAS JAMES, M.A. With 100 illustrations of JOHN TENNIEL . $1 25

" It is wonderful the hold these parables have had upon the human attention ; told to children, and yet of no less interest to men and women."—*Chautauqua Herald.*

" For many a long day nothing has been thought out or worked out so sure to prove entirely pleasing to cultured book-lovers."—*The Bookmaker.*

" These classic studies adorned with morals were never more neatly prepared for the public eye."—*The Milwaukee Wisconsin.*

XVII.—**Ancient Spanish Ballads.** Historic and Romantic. Translated, with notes, by J. G. LOCKHART. Reprinted from the revised edition of 1841, with 60 illustrations by ALLAN, ROBERTS, SIMSON, WARREN, AUBREY, and HARVEY . $1 50

" A mass of popular poetry which has never yet received the attention to which it is entitled."—*Boston Journal of Education.*

" The historical and artistic settings of these mediæval poetic gems enhance the value and attractiveness of the book."—*Buffalo Chronicle Advocate.*

XVIII.—The Wit and Wisdom of Sydney Smith. A selection of the most memorable passages in his Writings and Conversations . $1 00

XIX.—The Ideals of the Republic; or, Great Words from Great Americans. Comprising :—The "Declaration of Independence, 1776." "The Constitution of the United States, 1779." "Washington's Circular Letter, 1783." "Washington's First Inaugural, 1789." "Washington's Second Inaugural, 1793." "Washington's Farewell Address." "Lincoln's First Inaugural, 1861." "Lincoln's Second Inaugural, 1865." "Lincoln's Gettysburg Address, 1863." .   . $1 00

XX.—Selections from Thomas De Quincey. Comprising :—"On Murder Considered as One of the Fine Arts." "Three Memorable Murders." "The Spanish Nun" $1 00

XXI.—Tales by Heinrich Zschökke. Comprising :—"A New Year's Eve," "The Broken Pitcher," "Jonathan Frock," "A Walpurgis Night." Translated by PARKE GODWIN and WILLIAM P. PRENTICE.

In Preparation.

American War Ballads. A selection of the more noteworthy of the Ballads and Lyrics which were produced during the Revolution, the War of 1812, and the Civil War. Edited, with notes, by GEO. CARY EGGLESTON. With original illustrations.

French Ballads. Printed in the original text, selected and edited, with notes, by Prof. T. F. CRANE.

German Ballads. Printed in the original text.

G. P. PUTNAM'S SONS, PUBLISHERS
New York and London

www.ingramcontent.com/pod-product-compliance
Lightning Source LLC
Chambersburg PA
CBHW022000050726
47498CB00006BA/1993